Federal-State Relations in Unemployment Insurance

A Balance of Power

Murray Rubin

The W. E. Upjohn Institute for Employment Research

Library of Congress Cataloging in Publication Data

Rubin, Murray.
  Federal-state relations in unemployment insurance.

  1. Insurance, Unemployment—United States.
  2. Federal government—United States. I. Title.
  HD7096.U5R8   1983   353.0082'56   83-17118
  ISBN 0-88099-013-9
  ISBN 0-88099-012-0 (pbk.)

Copyright © 1983
by the
W. E. UPJOHN INSTITUTE
FOR EMPLOYMENT RESEARCH

300 South Westnedge Ave.
Kalamazoo, Michigan 49007

Foreword

For nearly 50 years the unemployment insurance program has functioned as a unique and largely successful intergovernmental effort. From its inception, federal and state governments have each had principal jurisdiction over particular aspects of the program and both have shared responsibilities for others. The distribution of authority and responsibilities has provided a balance of power which, in the author's view, accounts for the vitality of the program and its responsiveness to new problems over the years.

Rubin's concern is that recent economic developments and political shifts are producing an increasing federal dominance and a departure from long-standing program goals. From his analysis of the qualities and dynamics which have contributed to the UI program's past success, he concludes that the future of the program requires a return to the traditional federal-state balance of power.

Facts and observations presented in this study are the sole responsibility of the author. His viewpoints do not necessarily represent the positions of the W. E. Upjohn Institute for Employment Research.

Jack R. Woods
Acting Director

July 1983

The Author

The author, Murray A. Rubin, obtained B.A. and M.A. degrees at Rutgers University and later pursued graduate studies in political science at Ohio State University. In 1960 he joined the staff of the Unemployment Insurance Service of the Labor Department's former Bureau of Employment Security, where he specialized in state and federal UI legislation. As chief of the Division of Program Policy and Legislation, he was responsible for review of state UI legislation for conformity with federal law, preparation of draft legislation to assist states, negotiation with state officials on issues of nonconformity, and development of federal UI legislative programs. He retired from the Department after 29 years of government service. In 1979 he was appointed Consultant for Legislative Studies for the National Commission on Unemployment Compensation, where he prepared reports on a number of major UI issues. Since then he has contracted with both governmental and private organizations as a consultant on unemployment insurance.

Preface

This monograph reflects my association for almost 20 years with thousands of individuals in the state and federal employment security field. The accomplishments of unemployment insurance, this unique experiment in intergovernmental relations, are due in large measure to the skills and personal commitment of many of these public servants.

This monograph is dedicated to the memory of my first supervisor in the Unemployment Insurance Service, Philip Booth, who died in 1981. He is most representative, in my mind, of the "old guard," a diminishing group of outstanding federal and state civil servants who established the guiding principles of this program, and whose dedication served it so well for 50 years.

I wish to acknowledge my indebtedness to Saul Blaustein of the Upjohn Institute for his early support and continuing encouragement. This monograph has been much improved because of his many suggestions and careful editing. I am indebted also to my wife, whose patience, personal experience with the program, and typing skills helped see us through several drafts of this monograph. Errors and other limitations are solely my responsibility.

Murray Rubin
April 1983

Contents

Introduction

The unemployment insurance program has been successful by any reasonable measure throughout its nearly 50 years of existence. It has provided hope and help to millions of workers at critical times in their lives. Money for necessary expenses has been paid to qualified unemployed workers quickly, in an impartial manner, without a means or needs test and with relatively little fraud or scandal. Unlike welfare, which is based on a demonstration of need, unemployment insurance has not cost workers their self-respect. Its cost to employers, who finance the program, has not been negligible, but neither has it been excessive, given the value provided. The dollars pumped by the program into failing economies have helped workers and employers by forestalling potential economic disasters at both local and national levels.

These accomplishments have been made despite two apparent obstacles that seem serious enough to defeat any public program. While it is now accepted that insurance against unemployment is a legitimate governmental responsibility, the degree of protection to be provided is the subject of unremitting controversy, primarily between those anxious to ensure a high level of adequacy of protection and those for whom program costs, employer tax rates, and potential work disincentives are important concerns. This debate surfaces at least once every two years in the legislatures of all 50 States, Puerto Rico, the District of Columbia, and the Virgin

1

Islands, and not infrequently at the federal legislative level. Since each element of unemployment insurance—qualifying requirements, benefit amounts, benefit duration, eligibility and disqualification provisions, tax rates and financing provisions—has cost implications, proposed amendments to any and all such elements may provoke controversy. Over 2,000 unemployment insurance-related proposals are introduced each year in the states' legislatures. Not all are contentious, and not all controversy involves program adequacy versus program costs. However, those considerations underlie debate on most of the significant amendments.

But rather than being an obstacle, the cost-adequacy controversy has made unemployment insurance (UI) a dynamic program, responsive to economic and social change. When opposing views have been reasonably balanced, controversy and ensuing debate have usually resulted either in enactment of carefully considered legislation, or at least defeat of proposals that would weaken the program's effectiveness. When debate has been absent because of the dominance of either labor or management, the program has suffered distortions.

The second apparent obstacle also involves controversy. It arises from the fact that responsibilities for unemployment insurance are shared between two levels of government with different perspectives.

Each of the states and three other jurisdictions (called "states" for UI purposes) provides for its own complete, self-contained unemployment insurance program, administered by state employees. The states are responsible for all substantive matters: qualifying requirements; benefit levels; disqualification provisions; eligibility conditions; and tax structure. The federal government's responsibilities include maintaining nationwide standards which often include program matters. Friction results from state resentment of federal encroachments into state jurisdiction. It results also when state enactments or practices appear to federal officials to violate national standards. These issues of conformity with federal requirements are usually settled through peaceful negotiation, but occasionally they provoke heated confrontations. What makes conformity with federal standards compelling is the Federal Unemployment Tax Act, which provides for a payroll tax on virtually all employers. It allows employers to credit against most of the federal tax the taxes they pay under a state unemployment insurance program if that program conforms with federal standards. If a state UI law does not conform, employers receive no credit and are liable for the full federal tax, which may be considerably more than the taxes many employers pay under the state law. None of federal taxes thus payable would be used for unemployment benefits. Payment of both the full federal tax and state unemployment taxes could be prohibitive. Accordingly, the state would probably be forced either to abandon its nonconforming unemployment insurance program or find alternative financing. In most cases, denial of tax credit would be tantamount to elimination of the state's program.

Similarly, although the states are responsible for the administration of their programs, the responsibility for the design and nature of that administration is shared, since financing of UI administrative costs comes from federal funds. (A portion of the federal unemployment tax, which cannot be offset by state UI taxes paid, provides the source of funds for program administration.) Thus, state laws and practice also conform with additional federal controls (administrative standards and directives), if the state is to qualify for the funds necessary to run its program.

As indicated above, the result of this division of responsibilities is continual discord. The states seek independence from federal supervision over administrative matters and from federal intrusion into program matters. Federal administrations seek greater authority to establish priorities, ensure economical operations and exert more influence over program matters.

The intergovernmental conflicts, like the program adequacy-program costs controversy, have provided a "better product"—but only as long as the powers on each side have been reasonably balanced. Until recent years, statutory and practical restraints on the authority of both levels of government have helped preserve the balance by keeping each from usurping the powers of the other. These restraints and the resulting balance of state and federal authority have produced conflict, but more important, they have generated the high degree of intergovernmental cooperation that is necessary in order for either partner to operate effectively. This cooperation has been the key to the program's success.

For example, neither the federal nor any state government, given the awesome sanctions available, has any interest in provoking a conformity confrontation that could jeopardize the continued existence of a state's program. The result has been the resolution, through negotiation, of all but a handful of issues. Thus, despite an average of about 20 potential conformity issues being raised each year since the program began, there have been fewer than 30 formal conformity hearings actually undertaken over the first 45 years.

Another practical limitation on federal officials that encourages cooperation is their accountability to Congress. Amendments restricting the authority of the Secretary of Labor have followed past federal administrative actions considered arbitrary by a state-oriented Congress. That experience has been an inhibiting factor even during periods when administrations have been popular with Congress.

The states also face practical limitations on their authority that encourage cooperation and restraint. For example, certain past state enactments have been considered so arbitrary or discriminatory as to provoke congressional adoption of new federal standards. Each standard diminishes all states' authority.

The restraints on federal authority have allowed the wide discretion states have to tailor their programs to local conditions and preferences. This freedom has made possible the conflict and debate within state legislatures that have made state programs dynamic and responsive. The restraints on state authority have helped control state excesses and unwise legislation. The division of responsibilities and the restraints on both levels of government have necessitated the cooperation that has produced sound programs and effective administration.

It may be that other structural arrangements would have been as successful. A wholly state UI system would produce even greater diversity. However, without at least minimum federal responsibility, it seems likely that pressures of interstate competition ultimately would lead to serious inadequacies and inequities. A wholly federal system would have the advantage of greater efficiency that uniformity offers, but also the potential of sterility. Indeed, most of the innovations that have kept the unemployment insurance program current and dynamic have originated in the states, not from Washington, because of the opportunity for experimentation that the federal-state system encourages.

The balance of power produced by the division of responsibilities and the system of checks has always been fragile, dependent as it is on voluntary as well as statutory restraints. It has been seriously threatened in recent years. Increasingly, the federal government has tightened control over administration of the states' programs. More federal standards concerning substantive program matters, originally the states' jurisdiction, have been enacted since 1970 than during the first 35 years of the system's existence. Recent federal requirements concerning extended benefit duration have dominated that aspect of unemployment insurance and influenced regular program changes. Federal loans to bankrupt state UI funds and federally imposed conditions for repayment since 1974 have produced new federal influence over state UI tax matters.

There are as many reasons for the new federal dominance over the unemployment insurance system as there are manifestations of federal control. Preservation of the balance of power has been dependent on the states meeting their obligations and the federal government exercising restraint. Failures of the states to keep their programs current, adequate and solvent have contributed much to the recent federal invasion into matters ordinarily outside its jurisdiction. Currently (early 1983), insolvency is the most serious problem, with about half the states' UI funds in debt because of severe recessions, and more borrowers on the horizon. Federal restraint has been undermined not only by state failures, but also by inclusion in the federal unified budget of the Unemployment Trust Fund, through which all UI moneys flow, and the system's consequent vulnerability to national cost-cutting pressures.

The upset of the federal-state balance of power that has lasted nearly 50 years threatens the breakup of an intergovernmental relationship that has been both unique and highly successful. The full consequences of this trend are not yet clear.

The following chapters discuss first the original reasoning for the federal-state distribution of responsibilities and the provisions originally adopted to implement the system. They next describe later federal standards and their impact on the balance of power. The administration of the federal laws is explored, as well as the process of resolving conflicts. Finally, an assessment is attempted on the value of the balance to the system and the prospects for its preservation.

The intent of these chapters is to describe the federal-state division of responsibilities; to identify how the restraints on each partner's authority actually operated; to determine how and why they have been weakened; and finally, to evaluate the implications of increasing federal dominance. This effort seeks to examine the extent to which the federal-state balance of power has been important to the success of the American system of unemployment insurance.

Any light shed on this question should not only add to the understanding of the UI system, but also may have implications for other federal-state programs. In a period when new approaches to federalism are being explored, an understanding of the reasons for at least one federal-state program's success should be useful.

Chapter 1
Conceptual Framework
for a Cooperative System

Aside from those directly employed in it, few people are aware that unemployment insurance is a federal-state program. Even fewer have a clear idea of how responsibilities are actually shared. Nor is there much overt evidence anywhere of the division of authority. For example, when a laid off worker files a claim for unemployment insurance at the local claims office in Elizabeth, New Jersey (or any of the other approximately 2,000 local offices in this country) his interest is likely to focus only on whether he qualifies, how soon he can collect, the size of his check, and for how long he can draw. The worker may know that those objects of his concern have been subjects of debate in the New Jersey legislature. It's unlikely that he would know that these questions are also the subjects of an on-going federal-state tug of war that began in 1935.

From all he can observe, the Elizabeth claimant will assume that unemployment insurance is solely a matter between him and the State of New Jersey. The local office is a state-owned building. The claimstaker and all other UI and employment service personnel the claimant sees are state employees. The requirements the worker must satisfy are all spelled out in the New Jersey Unemployment Compensation Law. So too are the formulas from which the amount of his benefits is computed, the work-search and other tests of

9

availability he must pass, and the disqualifications that may be imposed on him. The unemployment check is signed by state officials and drawn from the New Jersey unemployment insurance fund, which is financed by UI taxes paid by New Jersey employers and workers. Not a whisper of federal influence appears to exist.

A federal worker employed by the U.S. Department of Labor's (DOL) Unemployment Insurance Service to review state UI laws for their conformity with federal requirements would see the program from a different perspective. She will know that New Jersey would probably not have enacted an unemployment insurance law as early as 1936, if at all, if the Social Security Act had not been adopted a year earlier. She will also know that the source of most major provisions of the New Jersey law, as well as the other states' laws, is legislative language suggested by the Social Security Board and later by the DOL. The local office operation in Elizabeth is paid for entirely with federal funds, including the salary of the claimstaker; federal funds finance, as well, the salaries of all other UI personnel in New Jersey and elsewhere.

Registration, reporting and claim filing requirements the claimant in Elizabeth must meet are governed by federal standards. A federal standard also applies to the time it takes the state to send the claimant his first check. If benefits are denied for any reason, the claimant is entitled to an appeal, as required by federal law, and the time within which a decision on the appeal can reasonably be expected is governed by a federal standard. If unemployment conditions are bad in New Jersey, the claimant may be entitled to as much as a 13-week extension of benefits, again because of federal law. From the federal employee's perspective, virtually every significant aspect of unemployment insurance is directly or indirectly controlled by federal law.

This example shows how thoroughly responsibilities are divided. It is hard to find another public program with authority so intertwined between two separate governments. The general lack of awareness of the existence of the partnership is perhaps a reflection of how smoothly it has operated.

Origins and Rationale

This chapter describes some of the thinking that led to the allocation of the basic responsibilities for the UI program between the federal government and the states. The division of responsibilities was incorporated into the original UI provisions of the Social Security Act which continue to dictate the structural framework of the American system of unemployment insurance. The most authoritative discussion of the reasoning for the federal-state division of responsibilities is contained in the 1935 *Report to the President* of President Roosevelt's Committee on Economic Security.[1]

The Committee recommended federal legislation to establish a federal-state system of unemployment insurance. Evidently, it did not consider seriously two other possible options. The first was retention of the status quo, which meant leaving total responsibility for unemployment insurance to state initiative. The failure of this approach was a principal reason the President believed federal action was needed in the UI area. As late as 1934, only Wisconsin had enacted a UI law. Even less realistic was another option—leaving unemployment insurance to individual employer initiative. Private unemployment benefit plans had developed very slowly, were quite limited, and many did not survive the early 1930s.[2]

The Committee considered a wholly federal UI program but rejected it in favor of a federal-state system for a number of reasons, not the least compelling of which was the fact that President Roosevelt favored such a hybrid approach. The Unemployment Insurance Subcommittee of the Technical Board (created to advise the Committee on Economic Security) decided at one of its first meetings to recommend a federal system. Its members, however, could not agree on specific provisions. The Subcommittee (and the Committee on Economic Security) ended by unanimously recommending a federal-state system.[3] In addition to the President's known preference for a hybrid system, the case for a wholly federal approach was weakened also because the constitutionality of *any* federal invasion into social and economic matters was still questionable, given the composition and tenor of the Supreme Court. It was reasoned that if unemployment insurance was structured as a federal-state program, the chances would be greater of its surviving the constitutional challenge. Finally, a wholly federal approach to cope directly with a problem such as unemployment was simply not consonant with American political tradition at that point—and it would not be easy to break tradition. Not only was a state-oriented Congress unlikely to relinquish all state authority over the issue, but also the founders and supporters of the Wisconsin unemployment insurance program had both considerable influence and interest in continuing what they had begun in 1932.

Although rejecting the wholly federal approach, the Committee still felt compelled to acknowledge the possibility that a future Congress may well find it desirable to abandon the dual government system entirely, "should those fears expressed by the champions of a federally administered system prove true. . . ."[4] Indeed, to remove possible roadblocks to future federalization should Congress follow that path, it recommended that the federal act require all states to prohibit provisions that would create vested interests in the current system and thereby tend to hinder modification or repeal of state UI laws if a wholly federal system was later enacted. Accordingly, as a condition for approval of tax credits, each state law must provide:

> . . . all the rights, privileges, or immunities confer-
> red by such law or by acts done pursuant thereto
> shall exist subject to the power of the legislature to
> amend or repeal such law at any time.[5]

According to the Committee, with such a provision in place,

> . . . the Congress can at any time increase the re-
> quirements which State laws must fulfill and may,
> if it sees fit, at some future time, substitute a
> federally administered system for the cooperative
> Federal-State system we recommend.[6]

The Committee recognized that responsibility for the nation's system of unemployment insurance would remain shared only as long as Congress continued to be convinced that the advantages of a federal-state balance of authority outweigh its drawbacks. An important advantage of a dual system was that it permitted wide latitude for experimentation by the states, needed because of the nation's lack of experience with unemployment insurance at that time. In the process, mistakes made by individual states could be confined within the boundaries of those states, while successful measures could be adopted and shared elsewhere.

The most serious disadvantage was that workers exposed to the same risk of unemployment would be treated differently from state to state, and the level of protection was likely to be wholly inadequate in some.

As noted elsewhere, recognition by both levels of government that Congress could alter the entire structure of the system at any time has been an important deterrent to abuse of authority, adoption of extreme provisions, and intemperate actions. Neither federal nor state officials have been anxious to jeopardize a partnership that has been successful by any reasonable measure.

As to the actual division of responsibilities, neither the Committee *Report* nor the Social Security Act systematically spells out federal and state duties in any detail. Instead, the *Report* contains general recommendations for five categories of responsibilities: providing an incentive for states to enact UI laws; adopting minimum standards for state programs; controlling reserve funds; establishing substantive program provisions; providing effective administration. In most cases, although certain functions were assigned either to the states or the federal government, the actual carrying out of the responsibilities proved to be a shared, not an exclusive, responsibility. Indeed, the single most pervasive theme of the Committee's *Report* is the expectation that the states and the federal government will find ways of accomplishing most unemployment insurance responsibilities through cooperative effort.

Providing an Incentive

The compelling need in 1935 was to provide an effective stimulus for state action:

> So long as there is danger that business in some States will gain a competitive advantage through failure of the State to enact an unemployment compensation law, few such laws will be enacted. This obstacle to State action can be removed only through the imposition by the Federal Government of a uniform tax (rate of contribution) on all employers throughout the country, so that no State will have an unfair advantage.[7]

The tax offset approach, by which credit for state UI taxes paid is allowable against the federal tax for employers in states with approved UI laws, proved to be an effective inducement. Prior to 1935, only Wisconsin had adopted a UI law. By the close of 1936, all but Illinois and Missouri had passed such laws and those two did so within the following six months. No state has ever voluntarily dropped out of the system by reason of not having an unemployment insurance law.

Tax offset is quite different from the more common grant-in-aid approaches that characterize many federal programs. The latter provide localities with an incentive to build airport facilities, for example, by providing funds either on a matching or other basis if the locality agrees and itself makes some effort. The tax offset approach acts less as a carrot than a stick since the main incentive it provides a state is an opportunity to avoid having the state's employers lose credit against the federal tax without any gain to the state.

According to the Committee, there was another reason why the tax credit approach was preferred over an approach under which the tax was wholly collected by the federal government and then remitted as grants-in-aid to the states. Under the latter system, the states would not have self-supporting laws of their own, "and as with all compensation having its source in federal grants, there would be great and constant pressure for larger grants exceeding the money raised by the tax, with a consequent confusion of compensation and relief."[8]

The federal law allows employers credit of up to 2.7 percent (90 percent of the original 3.0 percent federal payroll tax) for UI taxes they paid under a state law, provided that the state law satisfies certain federal requirements. The Federal Unemployment Tax Act (FUTA) tax rate, as of 1983, is 3.5 percent of the first $7,000 in wages paid by an employer to an employee in a calendar year. Employers subject to an approved state law continue to receive a maximum credit of 2.7 percent of the same wage base for state taxes paid. The maximum credit involves both normal and additional credit. Normal tax credit is credit employers receive against the federal tax for taxes they actually pay under a state law. An employer whose state tax was 1.0 percent of taxable wages would, therefore, receive normal credit of 1.0 percent. Additional tax credit (allowable only if the state law meets federal experience-rating requirements) is credit for the difference between what the employer actually paid and 2.7 percent. In the example above, additional credit would be 1.7 percent. Denial of both normal and additional credit means, of course, payment of 2.7 percent to the federal government in addition to the 0.8 percent balance already required.[9] The 0.8 percent balance collected by the federal government finances federal and state administrative costs, the 50 percent federal share of the cost of extended benefits, and a loan fund available to individual states with depleted unemployment funds.[10]

The tax offset approach provides a persuasive incentive not only for states to adopt UI laws that conform with federal requirements but also to cover every employer subject to the FUTA, and to establish their taxable wage base at least as high as the federal base. The reason for this is not because either is required for conformity. They are not. Aside from nonprofit organizations and state and local governments, which are not subject to the federal tax but which state laws *must* cover to be approved for tax credit, no issue of nonconformity with federal provisions is raised or sanction threatened if a state wishes to exclude certain employers in the private sector, or to exempt certain remuneration from its definition of taxable wages. But a state does neither employers nor workers any favor by excluding them from state law coverage or by reducing its tax base below that of the federal base. Since the employers are liable under the federal law for the FUTA tax, their exclusion under state law would result in denying them credit against the tax. In other words, the excluded employer would pay no state UI tax, but would become liable for the full federal tax (instead of the net 0.8 percent tax); the state fund would receive no revenue from the exempt employer; his workers would receive no benefits if they become unemployed.

For these reasons, there exists almost a complete overlap between federal and state coverage, and no state has a taxable wage base lower than the federal base.[11] Indeed, to avoid any inadvertent gap in coverage or tax base, DOL has recommended (and most states have adopted) provisions automatically requiring liability under the state law for any employer, employment or wages also liable under the FUTA or that the FUTA requires to be covered by the state as a condition for tax credit (as in the case of nonprofit organizations and state and local governments). Also for these reasons, coverage expansion and taxable wage base increases have occurred nationwide by reason of amendments first to federal law. Some states have always had broader coverage than the federal law and some have had higher tax bases. But most states usually have not acted independently in these areas. Without the powerful federal incentive, it is not likely that coverage would have extended to virtually all employees as it does today.

Shortly after enactment of the Social Security Act, the question was raised in the courts as to whether so persuasive an incentive as the tax offset credit approach constituted federal coercion. This challenge as well as other constitutional questions were resolved by the U.S. Supreme Court in 1937. Justice Cardozo, writing for the majority, rejected the allegation of coercion. A state has a choice:

> The State does not bind itself to keep the law in force. It does not even bind itself that the moneys paid into the federal fund will be kept there in-

definitely or for any stated time. On the contrary, the Secretary of the Treasury will honor a requisition for the whole or any part of the deposit in the fund whenever one is made by the appropriate officials. The only consequence of the repeal or excessive amendment of the statute, or the expenditure of the money, when requisitioned, for other than compensation uses or administrative expenses, is that approval of the law will end, and with it the allowances of a credit, upon notice to the state agency and an opportunity for hearing.[12]

In reality, when a state either enacts an amendment that puts it out of conformity with federal law or fails to enact a provision necessary for conformity, it jeopardizes the continued existence of its unemployment insurance program. If grants or tax credits were withheld, the results would be calamitous for the state's employers, workers, and probably the political leaders responsible. Thus, whether a state, as a practical matter, can choose to accept or reject the federal conditions for administrative grants or tax credits is certainly arguable. Yet legally, the states have a choice. State conformity is voluntary. Failure to meet a federal standard incurs no administrative or criminal penalty. The standards are not legally binding, and neither DOL, the courts, nor any other authority can coerce a state to comply. The distinction between practical and legal existence of a choice is important. As indicated above, the federal and state unemployment insurance laws survived their major constitutional challenges in 1937 on the grounds that the federal conditions were not mandatory. Over 40 years later, the constitutionality of the 1976 amendments to the federal law was sustained on the same basis.[13]

Adopting Minimum Program Standards: Federal Role, State Influence

If the first federal responsibility, according to the Committee on Economic Security, was to provide an incentive for all states to adopt unemployment insurance laws, the second was to provide certain minimum requirements where "uniformity is absolutely essential." The same tax offset credit approach that persuaded all states to adopt unemployment insurance laws also compels them to conform to the many federal requirements enacted and developed over the years. Thus for any employer to receive credit against the federal tax, his state unemployment insurance law must be certified each year as conforming to over 25 standards in the Federal Unemployment Tax Act (FUTA) which is part of the Internal Revenue Code. As explained below, for the state to receive funds necessary to administer the state program, the state law and its administration must also meet about a dozen additional federal standards in the Social Security Act.

All standards, many of which are cast in general terms, have been subject to interpretation. As a result, federal requirements including interpretative directives actually number many times the number of statutory standards. Any conformity with the standards must be absolute. A state may not, for example, meet the standard requiring coverage of state and local government workers by excluding temporary or part-time employees. It must cover all.[14] Failure, for example, of the Idaho legislature to cover members of the public Boise Symphony Orchestra created a conformity issue, not resolved until the state was persuaded to close the coverage gap.

Failure to conform with Federal Unemployment Tax Act standards means denial of tax credit. Failure to meet Social

Security Act standards means denial of administrative grants.

The federal government has authority, of course, not only to enforce existing standards, but also to adopt new standards as needed. The Committee on Economic Security recommended that federal standards cover only matters on which uniformity is absolutely essential. Congress has not followed that recommendation. The current variety of federal program standards, discussed in chapter 3, suggests the lack of any consistent guiding principle.

The Committee had recommended that the establishment of standards be a shared responsibility: "Some standardization is desirable, but we believe that this should not be a matter of Federal control, but of cooperative action." The statutory authority of the federal government to establish standards either by legislation or interpretation is unqualified, but in practice the states play an active role in influencing the fate of proposals that may affect them. Most standards have originated as federal administration proposals, and for most past administrations, no proposed standard was introduced without prior consultation with state officials and other interest groups that may be affected. Allowing states the opportunity to be heard did not always mean dropping proposals for standards to which they objected, but it did often result in improvements in the proposals, and this was a major reason why it was done.

In addition, state agencies are not without influence in Congress. The Interstate Conference of Employment Security Administrators follows closely all federal legislative proposals affecting the employment service and unemployment insurance programs. Administrators are polled on pending bills and their views are presented to Congress in testimony delivered during hearings on the bills by the Conference leadership. Individual state administrators have been known to lobby with their Congressmen on behalf of or in opposition to proposed legislation. In one way or another, Congressional delegations of states that would be either helped or disadvantaged are invariably prepared to react to proposed new federal unemployment insurance standards.

Controlling Reserve Funds:
Federal Role

The President's Committee on Economic Security placed great importance in the "intelligent and unified handling of reserve funds":

> Intelligently handled, unemployment reserve funds can be made an important factor in preventing a depression; but utilization for this purpose is possible only if their investment and liquidation is within control of the United States Treasury. We deem this an absolute essential if unemployment compensation is to accomplish the purposes for which it is designed.[15]

The Social Security Act provides for the establishment of an Unemployment Trust Fund in the U.S. Treasury; authority of the Secretary of the Treasury to invest amounts deposited in the fund in interest bearing obligations of the United States or obligations guaranteed by the United States; the maintaining of a separate bookkeeping account for each state agency; and authorization to pay out of the fund to any state agency such amount as it shall requisition. The provision is supplemented by sections of the Social Security Act and FUTA requiring deposit of all money received in the state's unemployment fund (except for certain refunds) immediately to the Secretary of the Treasury to the credit of the Unemployment Trust Fund. The establishment of the centralized fund and the requirement for immediate depositing into that fund by the states of all contributions would still not accomplish the Committee's objective if the moneys could be withdrawn by the states for any purpose. Accordingly, both the Social Security Act and FUTA prohibit expenditure of any money withdrawn from the fund for any purpose other than unemployment compensation (with certain minor exceptions).

The intent of these provisions was to avoid the funds being so invested or otherwise expended by the states as to jeopardize their availability for benefits when needed, or diminish their effectiveness as counter-cyclical measures. They constitute basic elements of the current federal-state system.

Federal safeguarding of the funds has not been seriously challenged in principle, but it has been a source of federal-state conflict, as described in chapter 2.

Establishing Sound Program Provisions: State Role, Federal Influence

According to the Committee on Economic Security:

> The plan for unemployment compensation that we suggest contemplates that the States shall have broad freedom to set up the type of unemployment compensation they wish. We believe that all matters in which uniformity is not absolutely essential should be left to the States.[16]

This suggests that the Committee envisioned the states as having very broad authority over program matters. The principal federal objective was to

> . . . stimulate the passage of complete and self-sustaining unemployment compensation laws in the States, by allowing a credit against the Federal tax for contributions paid under State laws.[17]

State independence was to be limited only in the few areas where "uniformity is absolutely essential."

The states never enjoyed quite the autonomy suggested by the Committee. Their "broad freedom to set up the type of unemployment compensation they wish" was circumscribed at the outset by federal law indirectly governing state minimum coverage and taxable wage base provisions and directly governing deposit and expenditure of reserves. Moreover, as indicated above, Congress never confined the adoption of federal standards over the program area to matters in which "uniformity is absolutely essential."

Still, the states had wide discretion over most substantive program matters: qualifying requirements; benefit and duration levels; eligibility and disqualification provisions; and tax schedules and rates. However, this discretion was of no immediate advantage. In 1935 there was an almost universal lack of knowledge about unemployment insurance. Very little was known at the state level about what was required to meet conditions for credit against the federal tax and what requirements must be satisfied to qualify for administrative grants. Under these circumstances, although a few states took independent action, most relied upon guidance from the federal government.

The *Report* of the Committee on Economic Security contained several suggestions for state legislation, later translated into a complete "draft bill." The Social Security Board prepared *Draft Bills for State Unemployment Compensation of Pooled Fund and Employer Reserve Account Types* which "meets the minimum standards set forth in the Social Security Act for State unemployment compensation laws." The Board emphasized, however,

This draft is merely suggestive and is intended to present some of the various alternatives that may

> be considered in the drafting of State unemploy-
> ment compensation acts. Therefore, it cannot
> properly be termed a 'model' bill or even a 'recom-
> mended' bill. This is in keeping with the policy of
> the Social Security Board of recognizing that it is
> the final responsibility and the right of each State
> to determine for itself just what type of legislation
> it desires and how it shall be drafted.[18]

Despite the disclaimer, most states had no realistic choice but to adopt large parts of the draft bills verbatim, with one state actually adopting all the alternative as well as the regular provisions offered. As a result, the original state unemployment insurance laws were quite similar. As Congress enacted amendments to the federal laws, the Social Security Board and later the Department of Labor issued new draft bills, now called *Manual of State Employment Security Legislation,* containing suggested draft language implementing the new requirements, as well as running commentary explaining the background and implications of alternative provisions. The draft bills and *Manual* are not confined to conformity matters. Neither the Social Security Board nor DOL has been inhibited in making recommendations to the state for adopting what they consider sound program provisions.

What differences existed among the early state laws were due largely to changes in successive versions of the *Manual* and in states selecting somewhat different nonrequired options offered in those documents.[19] A revised *Manual* was prepared usually every two years, with the last complete document issued in 1950. Since 1950, DOL has not issued a comprehensive *Manual* covering all aspects of a state law, but only suggested draft language designed to conform state laws to specific changes in or additions to the federal requirements.

Many years later, state UI laws are still more alike than different in basic structure and required provisions. Most contain identical language for provisions necessary for conformity, and there are now more required provisions than ever. But in nonrequired areas, there are now significant differences. These include provisions for qualifying requirements, weeky benefit amounts, benefit duration, eligibility and disqualifications. A review of several selected 1978 provisions of 13 representative states shows some of the more extreme differences.[20] A few examples of such differences, based on more recent data, include:

- A claimant with only about 5 weeks of work could qualify for 28 weeks of benefits in West Virginia in 1982, if his average weekly wage was as high as the average wage for all workers in the state for 1981 (about $277). In contrast, a claimant with only five weeks of work would not qualify for any benefits in most states. In Florida, at the other extreme, no claimant can qualify for as many as 26 weeks (the maximum) no matter how high his former wages unless he had 52 weeks of work in his base period.

- Two claimants with identical work experience can qualify for substantially different benefits. A claimant with six months' work at the 1981 U.S. average wage of $255 for production workers in private nonagricultural employment would qualify in 1982 for total benefits of $1,365 in Florida ($105 per week for 13 weeks) and almost three times that amount, or $4,050, in Pennsylvania ($135 per week for 30 weeks).

- Disqualification provisions also vary widely among the states. For example, in Kansas as of 1982, benefits were postponed a maximum of seven weeks for claimants who quit work without good cause. At the other extreme, the penalty for voluntarily quitting work could be as high as 25 weeks of benefit postponement in Colorado, with weeks of benefits reduced by the number of weeks of disqualification.

These wide differences suggest that the federal partner has been increasingly less persuasive in areas where it has no authority to insist. This is not entirely true. The DOL has been successful when it has been able to show the administrative or cost advantages of certain provisions over others (e.g., simplified benefit formulas), or when it has demonstrated clearly that some provisions are either substantially more equitable than others or more adequate in light of program objectives (e.g., indexing benefit ceilings to average wage levels; individual rather than uniform base periods and benefit years; reduction of waiting periods to no more than one week; increase of regular duration ceilings to 26 weeks). This is not to say that federal influence alone is responsible for the widespread adoption of these provisions. Certainly, the action and experience of other, particularly neighboring, states generally are more persuasive. It suggests only that positive and soundly presented federal advocacy at least provokes thinking about certain provisions and sometimes enhances their acceptability.

Achieving Sound Administration: Shared Responsibilities

The Committee on Economic Security intended for the states to have "primary responsibility for administration." However,

> To encourage efficient administration, without which unemployment insurance will fail to accomplish its purpose, we believe that the Federal Government should aid the States by granting them sufficient money for proper administration, under conditions designed to insure competence and probity.[21]

The states indeed have primary responsibility for administration. The program is administered at the state level, wholly through state employees, and with state facilities. The states even share in the development of federal administrative standards. In the past, DOL has actively sought advice and recommendations from state agency officials on proposed operations or performance standards. Many of these standards are the products of task forces and special work groups composed primarily of state officials. In developing these standards, usually DOL started with a commitment to the need for a standard and some idea of an acceptable level of state performance. Subject to DOL approval, the work groups developed such details as measurement periods, timetables, exceptions and penalties for failure to meet the performance goals.

Although the states may have primary responsibility for administration, and although states may sometimes be invited to share in the development of administrative standards, the federal partner has authority to control state administrative practices. The source of this authority is the federal control over the distribution of administrative grants and the power to establish standards "designed to insure competence and probity."

Under the Social Security Act, administrative grants are permitted only if the state law provides "such methods of administration as are found by the Secretary (of Labor) to be reasonably calculated to insure full payment of compensation when due." A second provision permits expenditure of administrative grants by a state only in the amounts and for the purposes found necessary by the Secretary for proper and efficient administration.

The virtually unqualified authority of DOL to allocate administrative grants[22] regularly collides with the states' responsibilities to administer their own laws. Control over allocation has translated into federal dictation of priorities, limitations on state flexibility, friction, and cooperation. The conflicts have produced state recommendations either for some share of the authority over allocations or for independent sources of administrative funds, without federal control.

There is some appeal to the states' claim for some control of that portion of the money from the net federal tax that has been earmarked since 1960 for administrative costs. This portion of the tax is collected from the employers in the state, transferred to Washington and then allocated back among the states. The result is less money for several states than would have been available if they had collected and retained the tax as state money, an approach advocated by several such states. But the money is difficult to justify legally as *state* money. It is derived from a federal tax for a statutorily prescribed purpose. Moreover, while many states would have more funds to use for administration if they collected and retained the earmarked tax on their employers, a substantial minority of usually smaller states would collect less from that tax than they now receive.

Many recognize also that state rather than federal collection of a tax earmarked for administration would not necessarily be an improvement. The state-collected tax would not necessarily flow automatically to the state agencies without state legislative appropriation and the oversight of state budget directors. State legislatures and executives could prove even more parsimonious than their Washington counterparts, particularly where controlled by individuals antagonistic to the state's unemployment insurance program.

Nor, in an era when money for benefit payments has become scarce, does it appear that relief from federal control over administration funds will come fron finding some independent source of such funds, as some states have urged, or from further distribution to the states of any excess of net federal unemployment taxes collected over administrative expenses. The so-called Reed Act adopted in 1954 provided that the excess of federal unemployment tax collections over administrative expenditures would be appropriated to the federal unemployment account until a loan fund of $200 million was accumulated. It also provided for the return to the states of any excess above the $200 million reserve, the excess to be used either for benefit purposes or administrative expenses including buildings (if appropriated by the state legislature for specific projects).[23] Excess moneys were actually returned to the states in 1956, 1957 and 1958. These Reed Act moneys became revolving funds in many cases. States that used them to buy buildings, for example, and were later reimbursed for those costs from administrative grants, thereby recouped their Reed Act credits and used them again and again. However, many states' Reed Act moneys were considered depleted when they were forced to borrow from the federal loan fund as a result of the 1975-78 recession. In order to borrow, all money available in the state fund for benefits, including Reed Act money, must first be expended. In 1982 Congress extended for 10 years the period within which any Reed Act moneys may be used for administrative purposes,[24] and also provided that states forced, in the past or in the future, to borrow money from the loan fund may, upon request of their Governor, have their Reed Act moneys that were considered expended for benefits restored and again available for administrative purposes. In any event, although the turnover of original Reed Act moneys seems perpetual, there is little likelihood that any further distributions will be made to the states from this source in the foreseeable future.

Practical Checks to Federal and State Authority

The foregoing discussion suggests that despite the many responsibilities allocated to the states, the statutory division of authority is overwhelmingly weighted in the federal government's favor. It is. In practice, however, federal and state powers have been roughly balanced. The reason is that the federal partner has neither the inclination until recent years, nor the resources to exercise even a small fraction of its potential authority. The inclination was weakened by inhibitions on federal initiatives represented by a state-oriented Congress. On three separate occasions, decisions holding state law out of conformity with federal requirements resulted in amendments to federal law either making the state practice acceptable or limiting federal authority over the issue. Federal officials are no more anxious to be in a position of imposing sanctions on states in cases of nonconformity than the states are to have them applied. This is true not only because success may be short lived, but also because the conformity process is a time and staff-consuming, frequently acrimonious process.

Nor are the resources available. Federal staff in Washington (UIS) now responsible for administering more standards than ever before has, ironically, steadily declined in recent years. In the early 1970s, UIS staff in Washington reached a peak of about 225, a figure then considered barely adequate even before federal standards multiplied by reason of 1976, 1980, 1981 and 1982 federal law amendments. As of January 1, 1983, authorized ceiling for the UIS was 113, with 105 actually on board—of which a substantial portion are clerical workers. State UI staff at the beginning of 1983 included a base staff of about 40,000, a figure that has remained fairly constant during the last few years.[25] As the National Commission on Unemployment Compensation observed in 1980, the federal staff is too small to perform even essential responsibilities competently, let alone monitor state administration to the extent necessary to ensure compliance with federal administrative and program standards.[26] No thorough review can realistically be made of each state's budget requests. Evaluation of a state's regulations and procedures is impossible given current staff limitations. There is not now adequate review even of the states' laws for conformity; nor is the rapidly diminishing pool of experienced workers being replaced by adequately trained individuals.

Budgetary restrictions on travel by UIS officials imposed in 1982, combined with a 400-1 state-federal staff ratio, virtually preclude the federal partner from providing even a semblance of the technical assistance to the states "in setting up their administrations and in the solution of the problems they will encounter," as recommended by the Committee on Economic Security.[27]

Another restraining factor is the presence of internal discord among the federal staff. The Unemployment Insurance Service is the DOL entity responsible for unemployment insurance. The UIS staff is divided among three groups of individuals with widely divergent views of the appropriate federal role. Dominant at one time, but now diminished in numbers and eclipsed in authority is a group of "old timers" who view the federal role as involving active leadership in introducing and promoting program improvements, and vigorous enforcement of federal standards. A second group, made up in large part of former state employment security agency employees, has substantially less interest in these activities than in assisting the states with technical problems and serving as a clearinghouse of information, particularly on administrative matters. The third group, now in the ascendancy, is composed of management-oriented individuals, with little background in UI, who are concerned less with preserving basic principles and concepts than with the cost effectiveness of the state agencies' operations. Although this analysis is an oversimplification, it serves to identify the major attitudes that compete for priority within a relatively small organization.

In addition, the UIS is frequently in conflict with at least three other DOL components. The Office of the Assistant

Secretary for Program Evaluation and Review (ASPER) with responsibilities for long-range planning has had recommendations on UI adopted by the Secretary (without UIS input) which were wholly inconsistent with long-standing Departmental policy.[28] The Office of Policy, Evaluation and Research (OPER), in the Department's Employment and Training Administration, with responsibility for coordinating the DOL employment and training legislative program, has occasionally conflicted with the UIS over appropriate strategy or Departmental testimony on behalf of federal UI law changes. The Office of the Solicitor (SOL) has frequently frustrated UIS efforts, as much by interminable delays in responding to requests for legal opinions as by opinions that counter UIS positions. These are not simply reflections of changes in political control of the executive branch, appearing first at higher levels and slowly working their way through the Department. The UIS has been responsive to political shifts, as any responsible bureaucracy must be. Rather, the conflicts reflect an unprofessional lack of coordination with UIS by separate organizational entities taking initiative in the UI area.

There are probably counterparts to these internal conflicts in most organizations. There is no reliable measure of their impact on the operations of an agency, and for that reason there is a tendency to disregard their influence. The fact is, however, that the existence of conflicting factions within an organization can sometimes be a determining factor in terms of particular actions taken or responsibilities abdicated.

All these factors have contributed to federal restraint. There are corresponding restraints on the exercise of state authority. It is generally recognized, for example, that when a state enacts a highly inequitable provision, or when it fails to update its law, or to improve its performance to reflect common expectations, it invites new federal standards. Some relatively recent federal restrictions—barring denial of benefits to interstate claimants, prohibiting cancellation or total reduction of benefit rights, and preventing denial of benefits to claimants in vocational training courses—reflect Congressional responses to demonstrably inequitable state law provisions. The adoption of a standard requiring all states to participate in a plan to give claimants who work in more than one state full credit for all their employment, and a federal standard, requiring minimum levels of state performance in issuing first checks and appeals decisions promptly, represent reactions to state inaction in areas demanding reform.

As important as both statutory checks and practical limitations have been in restraining federal and state authority, they have been less significant than another factor. This has been the realization on the part of state and, until recently, federal officials, that the most effective means of resolving problems connected with the program is through cooperative effort.

NOTES

1. The Committee was chaired by Frances Perkins (Secretary of Labor), and included Henry Morgenthau, Jr. (Secretary of the Treasury), Homer Cummings (Attorney General), Henry H. Wallace (Secretary of Agriculture), and Harry L. Hopkins (Federal Emergency Relief Administrator). Besides unemployment, this Committee dealt with economic insecurity resulting from old age, disability, death or absence of a family provider, and other problems affecting the welfare of families and children.

2. William Haber and Merrill G. Murray, *Unemployment Insurance in the American Economy* (Homewood, IL: Richard D. Irwin, Inc., 1966), pp. 61-63.

3. Edwin E. Witte, "Development of Unemployment Compensation," *Yale Law Journal,* Vol. 55, No. 1 (December 1945), p. 30.

4. *Report to the President of the Committee on Economic Security* (Washington, DC: U.S. Government Printing Office, 1935), p. 16. (This report hereafter referred to as Committee on Economic Security.)

5. Section 3304(a)(17), Federal Unemployment Tax Act. (Originally, all federal unemployment insurance law provisions were contained in the Social Security Act. In 1939 the taxing provisions of Title IX of the Social Security Act were transferred to the Internal Revenue Code by P.L. 76-1. The Federal Unemployment Tax Act is part of that Code.)

6. Committee on Economic Security, *op. cit.,* p. 16.

7. *Ibid.,* p. 16.

8. *Ibid.,* p. 17.

9. See also discussion in chapter 2 on experience rating standard.

10. An amendment to the Federal Unemployment Tax Act, enacted in August 1982 (P.L. 97-248) provides for an increase in the tax rate, effective January 1, 1985, to 6.2 percent of taxable wages, with a maximum tax credit allowed of 5.4 percent.

11. Some states have wage bases in excess of the federal and some cover employees not covered by federal law.

12. *Steward Machine Co.* v. *Davis,* 301 U.S. 548 (1937).

13. On October 6, 1980, the U.S. Supreme Court let stand the decision of the United State Court of Appeals for the District of Columbia in *County of Los Angeles, et al.* v. *Marshall,* No. 77-2138 and No. 78-1142. (See discussion of that case in chapter 5.)

14. Actually, Congress permitted states to exempt limited categories of occupations, described in Section 3309(b), Federal Unemployment Tax Act.

15. Committee on Economic Security, *op. cit.,* p. 17.

16. *Ibid.,* p. 20.

17. *Ibid.,* p. 17.

18. *Draft Bills for State Unemployment Compensation of Pooled Fund and Employer Reserve Account Types,* Social Security Board (Washington, DC: U.S. Government Printing Office, January 1937), p. 1.

19. Witte, *op. cit.,* p. 34.

20. Saul J. Blaustein, "Diverse Treatment of Claimants by States," *Unemployment Compensation: Studies and Research,* Vol. 1 (National Commission on Unemployment Compensation, July 1980), pp. 187-213.

21. Committee on Economic Security, *op. cit.,* pp. 18, 19.

22. Section 302(a) of the Social Security Act lists only three criteria to guide the Secretary of Labor in allocating grants: (1) the state's population, (2) estimates of coverage and administrative costs for the state, (3) such other factors as the Secretary finds relevant.

23. The original intent of legislative proposals leading to the Reed Act was to earmark federal unemployment tax receipts for employment security purposes. It was hoped that this would change the situation existing for many years in which the appropriation process produced less in appropriations for administration than was collected in federal unemployment taxes. See Haber, *op. cit.,* pp. 403-6.

24. Public Law 97-248, approved October 25, 1982.

25. Contingency staff, hired to meet heavy state workloads, has fluctuated from between 10,000 and 20,000 additional workers. For 1983, authorization of about 30,000 additional workers is contemplated in order to handle unprecedented workloads.

26. *Unemployment Compensation: Final Report* (National Commission on Unemployment Compensation, July 1980), p. 129. "The federal staff is too small to meet the responsibilities that go with a program of this size."

27. Committee on Economic Security, *op. cit.,* p. 20.

28. An example of this was ASPER's advocacy of taxing unemployment benefits for those whose total income exceeds specified limits; this position was later enacted in 1978 as part of P.L. 95-600 and more recently expanded (in 1982) by P.L. 97-248 by reducing the applicable income limits.

Chapter 2
Basic Statutory Provisions:
Conflict and Cooperation

Each of the unemployment insurance responsibilities described by the Committee on Economic Security was assigned either to federal to state authority by the original Social Security Act of 1935. This chapter describes how the Committee's ideas were implemented, what issues arose from the provisions of that Act, and how they were resolved. Later amendments affecting program standards are the subject of chapter 3. In implementing virtually all that the Committee had contemplated, the 1935 Act provided for every aspect of the system either through explicit statutory direction, or language sufficiently broad to allow a necessary flexibility. Above all, the 1935 Act established the division of responsibilities and, consequently, the balance of power characteristic of the system until recent developments upset the balance in favor of the federal partner.

Tax Credit Incentive

The first responsibility of the federal government—to provide an incentive for states to enact unemployment insurance laws—was effectively accomplished by the establishment in the 1935 Act of a 3.0 percent payroll tax and a provision allowing credit against that tax to employers for taxes they pay under an approved state unemployment insurance law. Originally, the tax applied to total wages. In 1939 its application was limited to the first $3,000 paid a worker by an employer in a calendar year. Only employers of eight or more workers in private industry and commerce were subject to the tax. In successive years, coverage was extended and both the tax rate and tax base were increased. The basic tax credit device itself has never been altered, and it remains a keystone of the system.

Control of Reserves

Another category of responsibilities assigned to the federal government, the safeguarding of reserves, was accomplished by two basic provisions that have not changed since 1935. They concern the deposit and withdrawal of state UI funds. The first requires states to pay all unemployment taxes they collect under the program "immediately" into the Federal Unemployment Trust Fund of the U.S. Treasury. This provides the federal government, as trustee of the funds, the means for preserving and protecting resources, one of the objectives of the Committee on Economic Security. Aside from an occasional dispute as to whether collected taxes are deposited quickly enough to satisfy the meaning of "immediate," this requirement has not generated serious issues.

The second provision adopted to ensure the safeguarding of reserves was the requirement that money withdrawn from the Federal Unemployment Trust Fund by a state may be used (with certain minor exceptions) only "in the payment of unemployment compensation. . . ."[1] "Compensation" is defined as "cash benefits payable to individuals with respect to their unemployment."[2] This restriction on what the states may spend their tax receipts for has produced considerable federal-state friction.

For example, state proposals to have claimants engage in community work projects and receive their unemployment benefits as "wages" were rejected by DOL as violative of the withdrawal requirement.[3] State officials argued for acceptance, claiming that both the community and the unemployed would benefit from the proposal—the former by getting important projects completed, and the latter by performing useful services and perhaps learning new skills.

DOL reasoning was that if benefits were conditioned upon claimants working for the community, they would not then be payable solely with respect to unemployment, but rather with respect to whether or not they performed such work. Even if the work was voluntary, as some states proposed, the requirement would not be met. Claimants performing community services would not have the opportunity to seek remunerative work. Thus, benefits would not be paid for unemployment due to lack of remunerative work, but rather to individuals whose unemployment was due, at least in part, to the fact that their engagement in community services prevented their search or availability for paying jobs.

DOL applied similar reasoning to state proposals to pay benefits to claimants out of work because of illness or disability. Claimants not able to work are not unemployed because of lack of work, but rather because of their physical condition. This interpretation of the withdrawal requirement was later modified somewhat to permit payment to individuals who become ill only after they file a claim. Benefits can be payable to them consistently with the withdrawal standard, provided they are not offered or do not reject a suitable job. The reasoning is that unless a claimant who becomes ill after filing a claim is offered a job, the unemployment can reasonably be considered due to the original cause of separation and continuing lack of work, not to the illness.[4]

Another modification of the strict application of the fund withdrawal requirement applies to claimants undertaking training. Even though a claimant in training may not have the opportunity to seek work, and may even refuse a job offer, DOL held that payment of benefits would not violate the withdrawal requirement. The reasoning was that by undertaking training, the claimant was demonstrating his availability for work. The training may be the most realistic approach the claimant can take toward obtaining permanent, meaningful employment. Some states continued to deny benefits on the grounds (used by DOL in other contexts) that a claimant who refuses an offer of suitable work or does not actively seek work because he is in training does not meet the availability-for-work requirement of the state law. The DOL approach prevailed by reason of a 1970 amendment to the federal law expressly prohibiting all states from denying benefits to claimants in training with the approval of the state agency on the grounds that they violate the state's availability, active search for work, or refusal of work requirements.[5]

The withdrawal requirement, that involuntary unemployment must be the sole determinant of benefit eligibility, has proved to be the major statutory bulwark in preserving the principle that unemployment insurance is distinguishable from relief,

> in that payments are made as a matter of right, not
> on a needs basis, but only while the worker is involuntarily unemployed.[6]

The requirement provided the basis for rejecting proposed state law amendments which would pay or increase benefits because of need, as well as others which would deny payment because of lack of need. A Wisconsin proposal was rejected, for example, which would have provided state extended benefits to individuals who exhausted regular benefits, provided they were in need, as defined in the state law on public assistance. Similarly, a New Jersey bill was considered violative of the withdrawal requirement because it provided a less severe penalty for voluntarily leaving work without good cause for individuals who could prove they were in need than applied to other claimants.

An Alaska bill, which provided that an individual with $7,000 in base-period wages would be required to serve an additional waiting week for each $1,000 in wages (up to a maximum of six weeks), was rejected as introducing a needs test rather than unemployment as the basis for paying benefits. The same reasoning was applied to an Oregon proposal to disqualify all workers who received wages and benefits during a calendar year totaling more than $6,000.

The withdrawal requirement was the basis also for rejecting a Washington proposal for a higher qualifying wage requirement for claimants who have a working spouse; a Minnesota proposal to put a lower ceiling on the maximum benefit payable to any secondary wage earner in a household with an employed head of the family; and a California proposal for limiting the maximum benefits paid to a husband and wife to one and one-half times the maximum payable to an individual.

The most persistent challenge to the withdrawal requirement is represented by a 1963 amendment to the South Dakota law, similar in nature to the Alaska and Oregon proposals noted above, requiring claimants whose base-period wages were higher than others to serve proportionately longer waiting weeks. The ensuing conformity confrontation is discussed in chapter 4.

Administration

In no aspect of the program, including the area of federal program standards, has federal control been more pronounced or provoked more friction than in the area of administration. As indicated in chapter 1, although the states have the responsibility to administer their laws, the federal government has authority over the administrative grants allocated to each state to assure that such funds will be spent "solely for the purposes and in the amounts found necessary by the Secretary of Labor for the proper and efficient administration of such State law."[7]

As if this authority was not enough, the Social Security Act also requires each state to provide:

> Such methods of administration . . . as are found by the Secretary of Labor to be reasonably calculated to insure full payment of unemployment compensation when due.[8]

This requirement is sufficiently broad to permit virtually any federal control over administration the DOL sees fit to impose. Control is not exercised through actual direct federal supervision of state operations or personnel. Federal influence is applied instead through development and enforcement of detailed operating and performance standards.

The claim filing standard, for example, describes in detail the circumstances under which claims must be filed, whether in person or by mail; the time the state must give a partially employed worker to file a claim; the kinds of job finding assistance, placement and other employment services that must be provided different categories of claimants, and defining such categories as ranging from workers on short term layoffs to persons permanently separated from their jobs.[9]

Operation standards similar to the claims filing standard and the claims determination standard, which concern activities connected with eligibility determinations,[10] cover the most significant facets of state administration of claims and many less important activities as well. Failure of a state to adhere completely to these detailed standards does not automatically mean that it violates the "methods of administration" requirement. If the state applies alternative provisions, DOL must determine if, in effect, they satisfy the federal requirement. If not, the state faces a conformity confrontation.

Distinguishable from operation standards, which dictate the procedural duties of the administrator, are two relatively recent performance standards requiring minimum levels of efficiency, as specified in terms of results. The appeals promptness standard, first issued in 1972 and later modified, prescribes as a minimum level of satisfactory state performance the issuance of at least 60 percent of all first level appeal decisions within 30 days of the date the appeal of an eligibility determination was filed and at least 80 percent within 45 days.[11] A state that meets these minimum criteria is considered to be meeting the standard.

If DOL finds that the failure of a state to meet the criteria is attributable to factors reasonably beyond the state's control and the state has done as much as is administratively feasible to overcome, the standard is considered satisfied. If the reasons were not beyond the state's control, recommendations are made for remedial action. Notice of an opportunity for a conformity hearing goes to the state in the event it fails or refuses to take necessary corrective actions.

The benefit payment promptness standard, issued in 1976 and revised in 1977, follows a similar pattern.[12] The criteria for minimum satisfactory levels of performance are issuance of 90 percent of first payments within 14 days following the end of the claimant's first compensable week claimed in the case of states requiring a noncompensable waiting week, 90 percent within 21 days for nonwaiting week states, and 95 percent within 35 days for all states. This applies only to intrastate claims (claims filed within a state by individuals whose benefits are based on wages earned in the same state). Separate criteria for interstate claims (filed by individuals with wages earned in a state other than the one in which they are filing) are 75 percent within 14 and 21 days with respect to waiting week and nonwaiting week states, respectively, and 80 percent within 35 days for all states.

The standard on payment promptness prescribes seven specific remedial steps to be taken by DOL if a state agency fails, "for an extended period," to meet the criteria or fails to show satisfactory improvement after having submitted a plan of corrective action. The first step is informal discussion with state agency officials. The ultimate step is notice to the state of an opportunity for a hearing on the question of whether the state is in nonconformity and, accordingly, whether administrative grants should be withheld.

The "methods of administration" requirement would seem broad enough to permit the federal government to dictate to the states any requirement having an administrative impact. Perhaps not anticipating the full interpretative potential of this provision, Congress explicitly included four specific administrative requirements in the Social Security Act. These concern the use of employment offices to pay benefits, selection of staff, information reports, and provision for fair hearing.

Payment Through Employment Offices

Federal law requires that the states pay unemployment benefits only through public employment offices.[13] This approach had been a recommendation of the Committee on Economic Security, but that Committee's *Report* contains no explanation of why this was considered necessary for efficient administration. It may have been intended to help ensure close cooperation with the employment service which has job referral functions and plays an important role in identifying work refusal and unavailability-for-work issues.

In any event, this requirement was the basis for one of the rare occasions in which a state was temporarily denied administrative grants. In 1939, grants to South Dakota were withheld when the state proposed to pay unemployment compensation through the state public welfare offices instead of through public employment offices. The proposal was advanced because no state appropriations had been made for the state's employment offices, to match federal grants for these offices, as was then required under the Wagner-Peyser Act.[14] The federal grants were restored after two months, when the state finally made money available to reopen the state employment offices.

Merit System Requirement

The Committee on Economic Security indicated that among federal conditions necessary to ensure competent administration, ". . . we deem selection of personnel on a merit basis vital to success."[15] The "methods of administration" standard in the Social Security Act was amended in 1939 to add the merit system requirement, though with a restriction on federal enforcement of the requirement, as follows:

> (including after January 1, 1940, methods relating to the establishment and maintenance of personnel standards on a merit basis, except that the Secretary of Labor shall exercise no authority with respect to the selection, tenure of office, and compensation of any individual employed in accordance with such methods).[16]

According to Frances Perkins' biographer, the language explicitly denying the Secretary authority over selection, tenure or compensation of any individual employed under a merit system was the result of Congressman (later Chief Justice) Fred M. Vinson's determination that "no damned social workers are going to come into my State and tell our people whom they shall hire."[17] The Executive Director of the Committee on Economic Security later gave credit to the Social Security Board's interpretation and implementation of the provision for giving great impetus to sound state administration by its insistence upon basing the selection and tenure of all employees in state employment security administrations on a merit basis. At the time, the great majority of states had no merit-based Civil Service systems. The Board required those states to establish special merit systems for employees concerned with employment security operations. This resulted in relatively competent staffing of unemployment insurance and employment service agencies and stimulated the passage of general state Civil Service laws in a number of states, based on a merit system. Eventually, there developed a large number of experienced employment security administrators and a strong tradition of nonpolitical administration.[18]

In 1970, responsibility for administering the merit system requirement was shifted from DOL to the U.S. Civil Service Commission. Established regulations governing state merit system requirements were substantially relaxed in 1979, particularly those identifying the UI positions that states were permitted to exempt from the merit system. The revised regulations provide that,

> To assure proper organizational responsiveness, appropriate numbers of top level positions may be exempted if they determine or publicly advocate substantial program policy, provide legal counsel, or are required to maintain a direct confidential working relationship with a key exempt official.[19]

The relaxation of merit system requirements is the result primarily of pressure from governors for more state flexibility; of the 1978 Intergovernmental Personnel Act (IPA), which requires that federal standards "shall be prescribed in such a manner to minimize federal intervention in state and local personnel administration"; of the declared position of the Carter Administration that governors shall be given maximum leeway in running grant-in-aid programs; and of the relaxation of regulations governing the federal Civil Service.

The result has been a substantial increase in recent years in the number of state agency positions exempt from merit system requirements. Another result, of course, is the absence of a single issue being raised in recent years of nonconformity or noncompliance with this requirement, in contrast with earlier experience of several of these issues being presented each year.

Required Reports and Disclosures of Information

The Social Security Act and the FUTA provide a number of information requirements of the states to facilitate administration and to authorize information exchange with other agencies:

> (6) The making of such reports in such form and containing such information, as the Secretary of Labor may from time to time require, and compliance with such provisions as the Secretary of Labor may from time to time find necessary to assure the correctness and verification of such reports; and

> (7) Making available upon request to any agency of the United States charged with the administration of public works or assistance through public employment, the name, address, ordinary occupation and employment status of each recipient of unemployment compensation, and a statement of such recipient's rights to further compensation under such law.[20]

The requirement of paragraph (6) is the basis for both regular statistical and special research reports from states. Under an established routine reporting system, state agencies collect and organize data from their UI operations for transmittal to DOL which summarizes and publishes the statistics for various purposes. Aside from the significance of the information for the purposes of managing and evaluating the program, much of the data, particularly regarding UI claims activity, are important factors useful in general economic analysis. In addition, weekly insured unemployment data are used to trigger on and off the payment of extended benefits.[21]

The reporting requirement of paragraph (6) has generated some minor issues. On occasion, states have resisted requests for special reports, usually on the grounds of insufficient staff. Some state agencies are habitually late in providing required reports. One state agency regularly does not respond or responds late and inadequately to requests for information concerning pending legislation. None of these issues, however, has been considered serious enough to warrant a conformity hearing. Paragraph (7) similarly has not produced serious issues, probably because the public works and work relief programs that now exist are administered at state or local levels; at the time this provision was adopted (1935), such programs were federally administered.

Another provision includes the following requirements for state agency cooperation with other federal agencies. Certification of granted funds is denied if the Secretary finds:

> (1) That such State does not make its records available to the Railroad Retirement Board and furnish to the Railroad Retirement Board at the expense of the Railroad Retirement Board such copies thereof as the Railroad Retirement Board deems necessary for its purposes; or

> (2) That such State is failing to afford reasonable cooperation with every agency of the United States charged with the administration of any unemployment insurance law.[22]

The foregoing requirements were either part of the original Social Security Act or were added during the very early years of the program.

Several additional disclosure requirements were added more recently. One requires disclosure, to a state or political subdivision, of wage information necessary for determining an individual's eligibility for (and the amount of) aid or services to needy families with children.[23] Another requires disclosure, to officers of any state or local child support enforcement agency, of wage information for the purposes of establishing child support obligations and locating and collecting such obligations.[24] A third requires disclosure, to officers and employees of the Department of Agriculture and of any state food stamp agency, of information concerning an individual's wages, application and eligibility for UI, name, address, any refusal of an offer of work, and if so, a description of the work offered.[25]

All the disclosure provisions require that the state agency adopt safeguards ensuring the information is used only for purposes of the programs for which it is requested. Authority to develop such safeguards for state adoption is granted to the Secretary of Labor in the case of the last two of the above disclosure standards and to the Secretary of Health and Human Services in the case of the first standard.

Provisions requiring disclosure of information to the identified agencies have not generated issues. The relatively new requirements should not create problems, provided the volume of requests from welfare, child support and food stamp agencies does not become excessive and the information requested is easily obtainable from existing records.

The absence of conformity issues under the foregoing provisions requiring disclosure does not mean that states are free of problems in this area. Many issues arise, not from these provisions, but rather from requirements prohibiting disclosure under certain circumstances. Both the Wagner-Peyser Act and the Social Security Act's "methods of administration" requirement have been interpreted as prohibiting disclosure of information obtained in the administration of the program from claimants and employers, if such disclosure would tend to deter individuals from filing claims, or employers from cooperating fully with employment security agencies. A state agency may not post the names of UI claimants on a courthouse wall, for example, or publish information about an employer that would help his competitors.

On the other hand, the federal interpretations permit disclosure (if consistent with state disclosure provisions) in a broad range of circumstances, including "disclosure to a public official in the performance of his public duties." Permitted disclosure is always conditioned upon it not disrupting agency operations, and upon the agency being reimbursed by the requesting authority if obtaining the information involves more than incidental expenses or staff time. Many states have had problems with excessive requests for the names and addresses of claimants, particularly from law enforcement officials. As a result, most states have more restrictions on information disclosure than set by federal interpretations, and all provide penalties for unauthorized disclosure.

Fair Hearing

One of the single most important of the administrative provisions included in the Social Security Act is the requirement that a state law provide:

> Opportunity for a fair hearing, before an impartial tribunal for all individuals whose claims for unemployment compensation are denied.[26]

This provision is categorized here as an administrative rather than a benefit standard. Its principal purpose is to require of each state the organizational machinery, trained staff including enough qualified and impartial referees, and all other features necessary to implement fully the right of each claimant who is denied benefits to a fair hearing. This right has been extended to employers who experience an adverse determination, on the grounds that this is necessary if the system is to ensure not only that benefits are paid to eligible individuals but also that they are denied to other individuals who do not meet the eligibility conditions.

The "fair hearing" provision has been interpreted by DOL over the years to require that any claimant or employer wishing to appeal an adverse determination shall be provided a hearing at a reasonably convenient location, at no expense, and with neither any obligation nor any need to obtain legal counsel. The hearing process must provide all parties at least the following due process safeguards.[27]

- Right to a hearing tailored to the capabilities and circumstances of those who are to be heard;
- Right to be represented by a person of the party's own choosing;
- Opportunity to present argument, to produce evidence and witnesses, and to offer evidence in explanation or rebuttal;
- Right to a compulsory process for obtaining necessary witnesses and records;
- Right to confront and be confronted by opposing parties and their witnesses;
- Right to cross-examine the other parties and their witnesses;
- Right to a prompt and comprehensive written decision giving the referee's findings, reasons, and conclusions, with substantial evidence obtained at the hearing to support them.

Each referee (the most common term used for state hearing officers) must understand and apply these due process rights, insure that the hearing and decision are completely intelligible to the parties, and obtain at the hearing all the facts necessary to reach a decision. Obviously, proper administration of this requirement is one of the most demanding responsibilities of a state agency. The key is a highly trained staff and effective management.

Under its "Appeals Performance Appraisal Project," DOL evaluates the quality of hearings and decisions by reviewing a sample of the written decisions and tapes of recorded hearings of one-third of the states each year. Failure, without good cause, of a state to attain minimum adequate levels of quality (established by uniform test criteria) constitutes violation of the requirement. Hearings and decisions are evaluated by applying several criteria and assigning specific points for "good," "acceptable," and "unsatisfactory" performance. The criteria include, for example, questions similar to the following:

- Was there opportunity for confrontation of all opposing witnesses?
- Was the language used in questions to witnesses geared to the comprehension of those present?
- Was the testimony taken in appropriate order and sequence?
- Did the decision contain the ultimate findings of fact required to resolve the issues in the case, and were they supported by the evidentiary findings of fact?
- Was the final decision of the referee clearly stated?

"Fair hearing" also means a reasonably prompt hearing and decision. As noted above, since 1972 performance standards have prescribed for the states minimum satisfactory levels of promptness. From the fair hearing and performance standards has evolved a system of informal administrative hearings unmatched by any other social program in providing fair, inexpensive, and quick determinations of issues for over a million appellants annually.

"Fair hearing" is not a static concept. For example, the National Commission on Unemployment Compensation (NCUC) has recommended deletion of two provisions, long standing in some state laws, which it considers violative of a fair hearing. The first denies a party to a hearing the right to be represented by anyone other than an attorney. The second prohibits any consideration of an appeal filed beyond the statutory time limit, regardless of the reason for the late filing. In addition, a minority of the Commission has argued that fairness requires the availability in each state of free and independent assistance and representation for claimants.[28]

The "fair hearing" requirement has been the basis of a large number and variety of conformity issues arising not only from violations of due process rights by state officials in conducting hearings, but also from state statutory provisions and proposed amendments. For example, a New Jersey interpretation permitting appeals tribunals to decide appeals solely on the basis of a review of the record was considered by DOL to be in violation of the fair hearing requirement because it gave claimants no opportunity to present testimony or arguments. An interpretation of a Wyoming provision, that a claimant must be conclusively presumed unavailable for work during any week in which he received a pension from his most recent employer, was considered by DOL a violation of the federal fair hearing standard; as have been other states' amendments establishing conclusive presumptions of ineligibility that offer no opportunity for the claimant to challenge.[29]

A claimant who fails, with good cause, to appear at the original hearing on his claim must have his hearing reopened, according to a DOL interpretation issued to all states.[30] And the fair hearing standard has been interpreted to require that benefit and eligibility hearings be public, subject to the limitation that the hearing tribunal must have authority to close a hearing involving matters of an intimate, or a personal nature.[31] DOL has consistently insisted that "sunshine" laws permit this exception to otherwise required open hearings. These examples represent only a small sample of the variety of fair hearing issues that arise each year.

Federal Program Standards

The Committee on Economic Security emphasized in its *Report* that unemployment insurance provisions in state law should be left entirely to the state legislatures in "all matters in which uniformity is not absolutely essential. . . ." This applied only to substantive program matters. Administrative matters required a cooperative effort; requirements aimed at safeguarding the fund, such as the immediate deposit and withdrawal standards, were federal responsibilities.

The Committee did not indicate any provision which it considered absolutely essential, but it was not reluctant at least to make recommendations as to what a state law should contain. Among others, it recommended relating duration or number of weeks of benefits payable to the number of weeks of prior employment; limiting benefits only to individuals both able and willing to work; providing additional weeks of benefits to individuals who have been long employed without drawing benefits; limiting benefits of seasonal workers to unemployment occurring within the usual season for their industry; and provision of partial benefit formulas which encourage claimants to take part-time or odd-job work when possible.[32] Most states adopted some but not all of these provisions. The following two Committee recommendations were incorporated into the 1935 Social Security Act as federal program standards.

Labor Standards

In the part of its *Report* titled "Suggestions for State Legislation," the Committee on Economic Security stated that claimants should be denied benefits if they refuse to accept suitable work. "Workers, however, should not be required to accept positions with wage, hour, or working conditions below the usual standard for the occupation or the particular region, or outside of the State, or where their rights of self-organization and collective bargaining would be interfered with."[33]

Although the Committee had not recommended these protections be imposed as a federal standard, the original Social Security Act required that each state include such labor standards in its law as a condition for approval for tax credit. These requirements were included probably to assure labor that unemployment insurance would not become a means of destroying unions or undermining existing wage, hour, and working conditions. This apprehension had caused the American Federation of Labor to oppose compulsory unemployment insurance before 1932.[34]

The Committee's recommendation was translated into the following federal standard that must, as a condition of approval for tax credit, be included in a state law:

> compensation shall not be denied in such State to any otherwise eligible individual for refusing to accept new work under any of the following conditions:
> (A) if the position offered is vacant due directly to a strike, lockout, or other labor dispute;
> (B) if the wages, hours, or other conditions of work are substantially less favorable to the individual than those prevailing for similar work in the locality;

(C) if as a condition of being employed the individual would be required to join a company union or to resign from or refrain from joining any bona fide labor organization.[35]

The purposes of parts (A) and (C) of these "labor standards" are to prevent UI claimants from being used as strikebreakers, and to protect the rights of claimants to join unions of their choice. Part (A) provoked a conformity confrontation with the States of Washington and California in 1949. The issue was whether workers who were separated *prior* to a labor dispute could be disqualified for refusing to return to their employer during the dispute. The Department of Labor held that the jobs refused constituted *new work* for those workers and that their disqualification violated the standard. The case was dropped when Washington changed its interpretation and California temporarily retracted its decisions disqualifying the workers.[36]

The issue led to a federal law amendment, sponsored by Senator William Knowland of California, restricting the Secretary's authority. Enacted in 1950, it stops the Secretary of Labor from finding that a state's interpretation of its law is preventing substantial compliance with the "labor standards" requirements until either the opportunity for administrative review of the interpretation is exhausted under the state law, or the interpretation is no longer subject to judicial review in the state.

Part (B) of the "labor standards" is intended to protect employed workers by preventing states from coercing claimants to accept depressed wages and working conditions. The provision is not easy to administer. It requires determinations of "new work," "similar" work, "prevailing" wages, hours and working conditions for similar work, and geographical boundaries of "locality." In 1950, DOL issued a 34-page detailed guide describing how the provision should be administered.[37] State claims and appeals adjudicators frequently still fail to identify a job offer as an offer of "new work," which can be either a new job or a change in conditions of a current job which constitute a change in the original employment contract. It is also still common to see the labor standards requirements confused with the concept of suitable work.

Suitable work criteria were intended originally to protect claimants by allowing them to refuse jobs without disqualification that were wholly incompatible with their ability or experience, constituted a danger to their health, safety or morals, or were too far away from their homes. Suitable work criteria were contained in draft bills of suggested state legislation prepared by the Social Security Board and its successors and adopted usually with little change by most states. In recent years, however, many states have narrowed the conditions under which a claimant may refuse a job because of its unsuitability. The most common change requires that after a prescribed number of weeks of unemployment, determinations of suitability need not take into consideration the claimant's prior wage levels, work experience, or training.

Suitable work criteria relate to the individual, while the labor standards (e.g., prevailing wage) relate more to the nature of the job or job market. Accordingly, a job that pays the prevailing wage and otherwise meets the labor standards may not be suitable work. Conversely, a claimant may refuse suitable work without disqualification if it is substandard in terms of prevailing hours, wages or conditions.

The most common conformity issue in this area arises from state amendments that ignore the prevailing wage requirement. Connecticut, for example, enacted an amendment to its law in 1973 which provided that a job offer shall be considered suitable if it pays either the prevailing wage or, "in the absence of a prevailing rate," a wage that is within 15 or 25 percent of the claimant's normal wage, depending upon whether the claimant had been unemployed six or more weeks or less than six weeks. Since a job that met these criteria automatically would be considered suitable, a claimant must take it or be denied benefits. The agency was advised by DOL that if claimants are disqualified for refusing a job that falls within the prescribed percentages but still pays less than the prevailing wage for similar work in the locality, the provision would present a question of conformity with the labor standards requirement (Part B, above). The Connecticut provision was deleted. There have been many such amendments and proposals.

Despite imperfect administration and less than universal understanding of the labor standards, these requirements have been important in preventing the unemployment insurance program being used as a vehicle for strikebreaking, depressing working conditions and otherwise undermining gains made by American workers.

Experience Rating Standard

Experience rating is intended to provide an incentive for employers to limit layoffs. Employers with favorable layoff experience in relation to payrolls receive lower tax rates than those with less favorable experience.

President Roosevelt had insisted that the unemployment insurance program promote employment stabilization, and experience rating appeared to be an appropriate vehicle for that purpose. The House had passed the Social Security bill without any experience rating provision on the grounds that by allowing states to vary employers' tax rates, such a provision would generate competition among the states in keeping employers' costs low. The Senate restored the experience rating provision partly because Wisconsin and several other states had already enacted laws with experience rating, and partly because a majority of the Senate Finance Committee subscribed to the concept.[38]

The Committee on Economic Security recommended leaving to the states the option of whether or not they would assign employers tax rates below 2.7 percent, the level necessary for the full normal credit against the federal tax. The Committee suggested that an employer assigned a reduced rate should receive not only the normal credit for the state tax against the federal tax, but also additional credit amounting to the difference between the actual state tax paid and the 2.7 percent level if the rate reduction was based on the accumulation of adequate reserves or on low unemployment experience. However, the Committee identified only two approaches a state might apply: it could permit particular industries or companies to have individual reserve or guaranteed employment accounts, or it could permit reduced rates on the basis of employers' favorable layoff experience.

The original Social Security Act and later the Federal Unemployment Tax Act permitted states to allow reduced rates only on those grounds. Although a few state laws originally provided for individual reserve or guaranteed employment accounts,[39] all states eventually came to providing reduced rates only on the basis of employers' experience. The Federal Unemployment Tax Act requires, as a condition for additional credit, that a state law provide reduced rates for an employer only on the basis of his

> . . . experience with respect to unemployment or other factors bearing a direct relation to unemployment risk during not less than the 3 consecutive years immediately preceding the computation date. . . .[40]

The law was later amended, first to permit reduced rates on the basis of as little as one year of experience, and later to newly covered employers "on a reasonable basis" (but not less than 1.0 percent) until they have enough years to qualify for a rate based on their experience.

This standard is important because it makes experience rating the *only* approach available to a state wishing to lower tax rates. Reductions in rates to levels below 2.7 percent cannot be made uniformly for all employers, or by any means other than the individual employer's "experience with respect to unemployment or other factors bearing a direct relation to unemployment risk." Under most state experience rating plans, this means that an employer's tax rate is keyed largely to the amount of benefits paid his former employees based on work performed for him.

Experience rating as a feature of unemployment insurance is unique to the United States, as is its federal-state system. All other countries with UI have uniform national programs and none establishes tax rates on the basis of individual employer's experience.

Once the experience rating standard was enacted, it has always had Congressional support. At the outset, many states did not provide for it at all, assuming they would need the full 2.7 percent or more to finance benefits. However, it soon became clear that costs were overestimated in many states and too much revenue would be generated. During World War II when unemployment levels were low, reserve funds accumulated in many states far in excess of amounts needed for benefit costs. Experience rating, which some states were reluctant to adopt, represented the only means available for reducing reserves. Although the degree of adherence to experience rating continues to vary widely among the states, Congress is committed to the concept. The recent rise, effective 1985, in the FUTA rate to 6.2 percent with a maximum tax credit of 5.4 percent seems designed to strengthen experience rating by forcing states to raise their maximum rates and thereby permit a wider range of rates. There is continuing controversy over the merits of experience rating, and these are better evaluated elsewhere.[41]

The important point here is that experience rating is mandated by federal law and has strong adherents despite recurring efforts to change or delete the requirement. In 1968, an administration-supported package of comprehensive UI changes (H.R. 8282) contained a provision deleting the standard. The proposal was opposed vigorously and removed from the bill in an early stage. The National Commission on Unemployment Compensation did not support a proposal by its Chairman merely to relax the requirement by giving states more flexibility. The proposal would have allowed the states to experience rate on the basis of "employment" as well as unemployment and to eliminate the requirement for a "direct" relationship to unemployment risk.[42] As in the case of every past effort to delete or modify the standard, the chief opposition came from employer representatives,[43] ordinarily in favor of eliminating federal standards.

The requirement, that any reduced rate be based on the employer's "experience with respect to unemployment or other factors bearing a direct relationship to unemployment risk," has been the source of much intergovernmental friction. DOL and its predecessors developed and applied very detailed and subtle interpretations of the standard over the years. So voluminous and complex were the interpretations that by 1950 it became necessary for DOL's Office of the Solicitor to issue a precedent manual on experience rating rulings "For Intra-Departmental Use Only." This "Experience Rating Digest" contains 50 single-space typed pages and well over 300 separate citations to formal and informal communications.[44] Until the comprehensive 1970 amendments (P.L. 91-373) which generated more issues in other areas, experience rating was the major source of conformity issues.

DOL rulings cover all aspects of experience rating—the composition of particular formulas for allocating rates, rate determinations for employers with gaps in experience, rates for employers involved in whole or partial transfers of business, and procedures governing group accounts. The Department has found acceptable many proposed factors for measuring employers' experience (e.g., separations, compensable separations, benefits, payroll declines) and has rejected others (e.g., the number of years the employer has been in business, the amount of taxes paid). The most common factor among the states is benefits charged to employers. The most common experience rating formula is the reserve ratio, under which the amount of an employer's reserve is calculated as contributions paid and credited to his account over all past periods reduced by the amount of benefits charged to his account during the same period. The reserve is then divided by the employer's recent annual payroll to provide a reserve ratio. The employer is assigned a rate in accordance with a schedule of tax rates associated with reserve ratios—the higher the ratio, the lower the rate.

An early Social Security Board ruling provided that not all benefits must be charged as long as those that were charged provided a reasonable measurement of an employer's experience with respect to the unemployment risk of his workers. This provoked pressure from a variety of sources for relief from charges, and noncharging of benefits was permitted under a wide variety of circumstances: benefits paid, without disqualification, to workers who quit their jobs with good cause not attributable to the employer; benefits paid following the serving of a disqualification; dependents' allowances; extended benefits. Some of the noncharging was permitted in the hope of easing pressure for more severe disqualifications.[45] Noncharging was justified on the grounds that the measure of each employer's experience would not be seriously distorted by relieving them of these charges, particularly in the case of benefits paid following separations not caused by the employer's action.

The rationale for certain other kinds of noncharging is not clear. There is lacking any coherent guiding principle and, as a result, rulings have been inconsistent. The Department of Labor has accepted noncharging of benefits paid for unemployment caused by a natural disaster, but rejected noncharging of benefits paid for other types of unemployment also caused by circumstances beyond the employer's control; e.g., the permanent closing of a mine because of the depletion of resources; the shutting down of a defense plant due to loss of a government contract; the dissolution of a business because of the illness of a partner. The Department has accepted as consistent with federal law a Delaware provision which provides some noncharging relief to employers who hire handicapped workers. Delaware, which considers the unemployed workers' wages instead of benefits in computing tax rates for employers, provides for disregarding, i.e., noncharging all wages paid to handicapped workers during the first 90 days of their employment. The Department, however, has barred similar relief from charges for employers for hiring veterans or minorities, or for participating in programs aimed at employing youth and other targeted groups. The Department permits no distinctions based on industrial classification or employer size in assigning reduced rates (except for new employers).

Other than the experience rating requirements, states are under no restrictions concerning the assignment of rates. States are free, for example, to set rates higher than the standard rate on any basis they choose. Accordingly, although all states have minimum and maximum rates, these vary widely among states. Tax bases also vary, so that *effective* tax rates (the tax payable as a proportion of total payroll) may be different even for employers with identical experience and identical rates in different states. No two tax structures are the same.

The inconsistencies in rulings and lack of guiding principles make DOL positions vulnerable. There have been relatively few conflicts over experience rating in recent years only because the Unemployment Insurance Service has been preoccupied with an avalanche of issues arising from new legislation. It has ignored state law amendments that in past years would have provoked conformity confrontations. Fortunately, the great majority of experience rating issues arise over obscure provisions that have little or no significant impact on the program.

State Programs

The original Act followed the example of the Tenth Amendment to the Constitution by providing, at least implicitly, that all unemployment insurance responsibilities not expressly delegated or implied to the federal government are reserved to the states. While the states were required to adhere to such basic requirements as those relating to deposit and withdrawal of tax moneys, and to conform with other federal requirements, originally there were relatively few such requirements governing administrative matters (merit system, fair hearing, payment through employment offices, disclosure) before extensive interpretations were made of the "methods of administration" requirement. Only two federal program standards ("labor standards," experience rating standards) inhibited state action in this area.

As described in chapter 1, originally the most significant restraint on state autonomy in the program area was ignorance of what an unemployment insurance law should contain and consequent dependence on federal guidance. States gradually acquired more experience and thereby more independence, and concurrently, the federal government developed more interpretations of existing statutory requirements, particularly in the administration and experience rating areas. These developments were somewhat inevitable since reactions were needed to issues and new state provisions constantly arising during the early years.

The interpretation approach, in contrast to the later reliance on enactment of federal standards, proved compatible with the federal-state balance of authority. Federal interpretations were addressed to particular problems, developed usually from a sound legal basis, and designed to be consistent with basic objectives of unemployment insurance. This was not always true with enactment of federal program standards. Equally important, interpretations of federal law were more easily subject than federal law amendments to successful challenge by the states—often before they became effective. Finally, interpretations were more likely than statutory enactments to be the product of cooperative effort, and consequently, more likely to represent realistic solutions to problems. In effect, the basic structure provided by the original Social Security Act permitted both state and federal jurisdictions the flexibility necessary to allow state UI programs to adjust to changing conditions while continuing to serve fundamental principles.

NOTES

1. Section 303(a)(5), Social Security Act (SSA).

2. Section 3306(h), Federal Unemployment Tax Act (FUTA).

3. Letter, Governor James B. Longley, Maine to William Kolberg, Assistant Secretary for Manpower, October 24, 1975, for example, asked approval of proposal to permit unemployment insurance claimants to work on public works projects while drawing benefits.

4. Social Security Board action on a proposed Maryland amendment, January 4, 1945.

5. Section 3304(a)(8), FUTA.

6. Margaret M. Dahm and Phyllis H. Fineshriber, "Examining Dependents' Allowances," *Unemployment Compensation: Studies and Research*, Vol. 1 (National Commission on Unemployment Compensa-

tion, July 1980), Appendix A: Entitlement to Unemployment Benefits Based on Consideration Involving Need: Conformity with Requirements of Federal Law, pp. 84-87. Examples in ensuing paragraphs also drawn from this source.

7. Section 303(a)(8), SSA.

8. Section 303(a)(1), SSA.

9. *Standard for Claim Filing, Claimant Reporting, Job Finding, and Employment Services,* Part V, Section 5000-5999, Employment Security Manual, Revised August 31, 1970.

10. *Standard for Claim Determinations—Separation Information,* Part V, Section 6000-6999, Employment Security Manual, Revised October 28, 1968.

11. *Appeals Promptness Standard,* Part 650.1-.5, Chapter V, Title 20, Code of Federal Regulations.

12. *Standard for Benefit Payment Promptness,* Part 640, Chapter V, Title 20, Code of Federal Regulations, July 28, 1978.

13. Section 3304(a)(1), FUTA and Section 303(a)(2), SSA, currently provide, "all compensation is to be paid through public employment offices or such other agencies as the Secretary of Labor may approve."

14. Frank Traver De Vyver, "Federal Standards in Unemployment Insurance," *Vanderbilt Law Review,* Vol. 8, No. 2 (February 1955), pp. 421, 422. The Wagner-Peyser Act, adopted in 1933, provided for a nationwide employment service consisting of state administered public employment offices affiliated with the U.S. employment service and financed on a joint federal-state basis.

15. Committee on Economic Security, *op. cit.,* p. 19.

16. Section 303(a)(1), SSA.

17. George Martin, *Madam Secretary Frances Perkins* (Boston: Houghton Mifflin Co., 1976), p. 355.

18. Edwin E. Witte, "Development of Unemployment Compensation," *Yale Law Journal,* Vol. 55, No. 1 (December 1945), p. 37.

19. Revised Regulations, Office of Personnel Management, U.S. Civil Service Commission, 1979.

20. Sections 303(a)(6) and (7), SSA.

21. A maximum of 13 weeks of extended benefits is payable to qualified claimants under the Federal-State Extended Unemployment Compensation Act of 1970 (P.L. 91-373) when insured unemployment rates in a state reach levels high enough to "trigger on" the availability of these

benefits and cease to be payable when the level of insured unemployment drops sufficiently to "trigger off" their availability. See discussion of extended benefits in chapter 3.

22. Section 303(c), SSA.

23. Section 303(a)(6), SSA, Public Law 95-216, approved December 20, 1977.

24. Section 303(d), SSA, Social Security Disability Amendments of 1980, effective January 1, 1983.

25. Section 303(e), SSA, Food Stamp Amendments of 1980, effective January 1, 1983.

26. Section 303(a)(3), SSA.

27. *Unemployment Compensation: Final Report* (National Commission on Unemployment Compensation, July 1980), p. 116. See also *A Guide to Unemployment Insurance Benefit Appeals—Principles and Procedures* (U.S. Department of Labor, January 1970).

28. *Unemployment Compensation: Final Report, op. cit.,* p. 120.

29. See De Vyver, *op. cit.,* p. 418, for New Jersey and Wyoming examples.

30. *A Guide to Unemployment Insurance Benefit Appeals—Principles and Procedures* (U.S. Department of Labor, January 1970), p. 25.

31. *Ibid.,* p. 21.

32. Committee on Economic Security, *op. cit.,* pp. 20, 21.

33. *Ibid.,* p. 21.

34. William Haber and Merrill G. Murray, *Unemployment Insurance in the American Economy* (Homewood, IL: Richard D. Irwin, Inc., 1966), p. 83.

35. Section 3304(a)(5), FUTA.

36. See discussion of California and Washington cases under *Labor Standards Issues* in chapter 5.

37. U.S. Department of Labor, Bureau of Employment Security, Unemployment Compensation Program Letter No. 130, *Principles Underlying the Prevailing Conditions of Work Standard,* January 6, 1947, reissued September 1950.

38. Haber, *op. cit.,* pp. 331-2.

39. Under the guaranteed employment account, separate accounts are maintained for each employer who guarantees in advance at least 30 hours of work for each of 40 weeks to all his employees who continue to

be eligible for suitable work. The employer must assure that from the separate account will be paid benefits to former employees whose guaranteed remuneration has not been paid or whose guarantee is not renewed. Under the reserve account system, a separate account is maintained for each employer from which benefits are paid on the basis of work performed for the employer. Paragraphs (2) and (3) of section 3303(a), FUTA, prescribe minimum account balances and other preconditions to reduced rates. The guaranteed employment approach was never adopted by a single state. Seven states adopted the employer reserve type of fund.

40. Section 3303(a)(1), FUTA.

41. See Joseph M. Becker, S.J., *Experience Rating in Unemployment Insurance: Virtue or Vice* (Kalamazoo, MI: The W.E. Upjohn Institute for Employment Research, 1972). See also: Haber, *op. cit.,* pp. 330-357.

42. *Unemployment Compensation: Final Report, op. cit.,* p. 94.

43. Haber, *op. cit.,* p. 356.

44. U.S. Department of Labor, Office of the Solicitor, *Experience Rating Digest,* 1950.

45. U.S. Department of Labor, Bureau of Employment Security, Unemployment Compensation Program Letter, No. 78, December 29, 1944.

Chapter 3
Federal Program Standards:
Weakening the Balance

The states have never been entirely free to enact "complete and self-sustaining" unemployment insurance laws covering "all matters in which uniformity is not absolutely essential . . . ," as recommended by the Committee on Economic Security. The original Social Security Act included federal requirements covering the maintenance of tax funds, distribution of administrative responsibilities and other provisions establishing the system's structural framework. In addition to these "structural" requirements, the original act contained two program standards. The "labor standards" requirement barred states from disqualifying claimants for refusing an offer of new work which was substandard or which prevented them from joining a union of their choice. The experience rating standard permitted states to assign reduced UI tax rates to employers only on the basis of their experience with unemployment.

These two original program standards, the "structural" requirements outlined above, and interpretations of all these provisions, remained the only federal requirements for 35 years. The program standards described in this chapter were added in 1970, 1976, 1980, 1981 and 1982. They vary widely in terms of their impact on the program. Each diminished the scope of state autonomy over the program area and, to that degree, also weakened the federal-state balance. In most cases, it is questionable that this result was offset by any benefit the standard brought to the program. Their discussion here is organized according to their prevailing motivation: to protect the rights of claimants, and to restrict benefits rights to the "deserving" claimants. A third category includes two complex standards that contain requirements aimed at both these objectives. Each standard is examined in terms of the problem that produced it and the issues it has presented. For very few of these program standards can it reasonably be argued that uniformity imposed by federal law was "absolutely essential" (the Committee's criterion). Most were enacted, not because uniformity was necessary, but simply to supersede certain state provisions Congress considered either too harsh in their impact on claimants or too lenient. The latest standards were also the products of two developments: inclusion of the unemployment trust fund in the federal budget; and the financial crises of the 1970s and early 1980s. The first made UI a potential target for federal budget cutting efforts. The second provided the motive for actual federal and state cost reduction enactments.

Standards that Protect Claimants

Protection of Interstate Claimants

One of the perplexing problems faced by the Committee on Economic Security was that posed by workers who move from state to state. Under a strictly national system, all workers could be treated the same; but under a system involving largely autonomous state programs, the interstate worker could be left without protection. Soon after the system began, the states developed a plan under which each state would act as the agent for other states which were liable for benefits claimed by workers based on employment and earnings in the liable state but who moved to the agent state.

The agent state took the claims of such workers for the liable state. All states participated in this plan. Other interstate plans allowed a worker to combine wages earned in two or more states if the wages earned in any one state were not sufficient to qualify the claimant for benefits or if combining would result in higher benefits. Not all states participated in the combined wage plans. The result was that interstate claimants were treated differently in different states.

In 1970, federal law was amended to require that all states "shall participate" in a plan which combines the wages and employment of an individual who worked in more than one state so that eligibility for and amount of benefits could be based on the combined wages and work when applying the provisions of a single state.[1] This standard did not produce issues of conformity with any state, but it did generate a number of technical issues. One question, for example, concerned liability for benefit charges to an employer's experience rating account when a claimant's wage credits earned with that employer are transferred to another state for combining purposes but are insufficient alone to qualify that claimant in the transferring state.[2]

A second standard affecting interstate claimants was also adopted in 1970.[3] It too resulted from the failure of some states to treat claimants equitably. In 1963 Ohio and Wyoming provided that an interstate claimant filing against these states may not qualify for a maximum higher than that payable in the agent state where they file their claim. Alaska, as early as 1955, provided a maximum of $45 to claimants filing within the state but a maximum of $25 to claimants who filed claims against Alaska from outside the state. Dependents' allowances were payable only for dependents residing in Alaska.

These discriminatory provisions were characterized by a Congressional Committee as:

> . . . not only inequitable to the individual claimant and injurious to the proper functioning of the unemployment insurance system but inhibit among workers a very desirable mobility which is important to our economy.[4]

The enacted federal standard bars states from denying or reducing benefits to an individual solely because the claim is filed from another state (or Canada) or because of a change in residence to another state (or Canada) where the claim is filed.[5] Ironically, the only exception to this federal ban on discrimination against interstate claimants is another federal provision enacted ten years later. That provision amended the extended benefits program by prohibiting payment of more than two weeks of extended benefits if the claimant filed from a state where an extended benefit period was not in effect.[6]

It may be argued that the failure of some states to participate in combined wage plans and the enactment by others of discriminatory provisions made federal intervention inevitable. It is possible that, as their economies declined, more and more states would have followed Alaska's example. Representatives of that state argue that individuals who work in Alaska, often in seasonal jobs, and then move south represent a drain on the state's economy. Their unemployment benefit checks reflect high seasonal wages and an economy with a high cost of living. When they move to lower cost states, there may be little incentive to work for wages that compare unfavorably with their unemployment benefits. There may also be less incentive for an agent state to test the availability or develop job openings for an interstate claimant than for an intrastate claimant drawing benefits from the agent state's fund.

The foregoing may be true in some situations, but the pattern is not characteristic of interstate claimants. There are sound reasons why each year thousands of workers move from one state to another. In any event, the remedy to abuses of the system by interstate claimants would seem to lie in improved administration of the interstate program. This is also the remedy for the unequal treatment interstate claimants continue to receive despite the federal standards. As noted in chapter 2, their claims are processed and paid more slowly than intrastate claims, and their appeals also take longer to complete. The delays are partly the result of the additional processing necessary for an interstate claim, but most of the unequal treatment is attributable to failure of the federal partner consistently to insist upon promptness as well as equal administration of these claims.

Among all the standards intended to protect claimants against unfair disqualification, a strong case can be made that those relating to interstate claimants provide a needed uniform protection. It may be, however, that even those standards would not have been necessary, given reasonable interpretations of the original Social Security Act. For example, if the "withdrawal-of-funds standard" can be interpreted as barring payment or denial of benefits on the basis of need, presumably it could also have been interpreted as barring discrimination against interstate claimants. The same reasoning would seem to apply: under both situations, benefits would be paid or denied on a basis other than the claimant's unemployment due to lack of work. It would seem feasible also that the "methods of administration" requirement in the original Act could have been interpreted as requiring all states to participate in a uniform combined wage plan. In any event, the results would have been the same. The only point is that they (and perhaps better results) could have been achieved earlier through interpretation than by enactment of new standards.

Protection of Claimants Taking Training

The Department of Labor had long encouraged states to provide training and retraining for claimants who would benefit from new skills. The experience rating standard was interpreted to permit states to relieve employers of charges for benefits paid claimants engaged in approved training. Benefits paid a claimant taking training were considered benefits paid for unemployment even though the claimant might be unavailable for work by reason of the training, and even though he may refuse a suitable job because it interfered with his training. Not all states subscribed to this position. Several disqualified claimants in training for refusing work and some held them unavailable if the training precluded an active search for work.

The federal standard adopted by Congress in 1970 bars the states from disqualifying claimants in approved training on the grounds that they are unavailable, are not making an active search for work, or have refused an offer of suitable work.[7] According to the Senate Finance Committee Report on the 1970 amendments, these provisions "should not be used to discourage claimants from entering training which has been approved by the state agencies.[8] In commenting on the new requirement, DOL recommended that states develop regulations to assure that before approval, it is established that the training will enhance the claimant's employability. It advised, however, that under the requirement, "each state is free to determine what training is appropriate for a claimant, what criteria are established for approval of training for an individual, and what safeguards are established to assure that the claimant for whom the training has been approved is actually attending such training."[9]

Few issues have been presented by this federal standard because not all states actually developed criteria for approving an individual for training, and not many unemployment insurance claimants are involved in training or retraining anyway. The federal requirement may be circumvented easily by a state either refusing to approve training for any claimant, or setting prohibitive conditions on the approval of training.

A potential issue was presented by a number of state laws which deny benefits to claimants taking any training providing cash or other allowances. Since an individual taking Comprehensive Employment and Training Act (CETA) training (which usually paid allowances) had approval of the state employment security agency, it was argued within DOL that the state laws denying benefits to claimants taking allowance-paying training were inconsistent with the UI training standard. However, the issue was never raised.

Protection Against Excessive Penalties

Another standard aimed at protecting claimants from unreasonable penalties was a reaction to a trend toward increasingly severe disqualifications. For many years, DOL fought a losing battle in this area, trying to persuade the states of the advantages of limiting disqualifications to a postponement of benefits for about six weeks (the national average duration of a spell of unemployment). In 1944 the experience rating standard was interpreted to permit states to noncharge employers for benefits paid following a disqualification. It was hoped that this would help ease the pressure for harsher disqualifications.[10]

The standard enacted in 1970 prohibits states from cancelling the wage credits (earnings on which benefits are based) or completely eliminating the benefit rights of any individual disqualified for any cause except discharge for misconduct connected with the work, fraud in connection with a claim, or receipt of disqualifying income.[11] According to the Senate Finance Committee Report,

> This proposal is directed solely to the preservation, in all but the excepted cases, of some portion of an individual's monetary entitlement for his benefit year, the "bank account" of benefits against which, if otherwise eligible, he can draw. The requirement would affect only those few State laws which cancel wage credits or totally reduce benefits.[12]

Although the standard caused a few states to amend their laws, it actually represents a very modest restraint on states. The provision in no way restricts states in establishing any conditions it sees fit as eligibility requirements for benefits. It does not prevent any state from increasing the number or type of infractions for which a disqualification may be applied. It does not really inhibit, in any significant way, a state from imposing as severe a disqualification as it wishes for any cause. The provision does not preclude a disqualification for the duration of the claimant's unemployment and until the claimant obtains another job, works at least a prescribed minimum period, earns at least a specified minimum amount and is then separated from the job for nondisqualifying reasons. This is permitted under the standard, even though failure to obtain another job is tantamount to complete denial of benefits. Most states now apply such a disqualification for one or all of the major causes of disqualification.

The standard prohibits *any* cancellation of wage credits (except in the three specified situations). This means the state may not cancel for benefit purposes wages earned from an employer from whom the claimant separated under disqualifying conditions. The standard bars only "total" reduction of benefit rights. Cancellation of wage credits may not be as severe a penalty as reduction of benefit rights, particularly for claimants with more than one base-period employer. For example, a state may be consistent with the standard if, in the case of a claimant otherwise entitled to 26 weeks of benefits, it disqualifies the claimant for 25 weeks, with an equal reduction in benefits. Since this leaves the claimant with one week of benefits, and thus preserves "some portion of an individual's monetary entitlement," it satisfies the standard. The impact of such a disqualification is denial of all but one week of benefits for a year, not only six months. This is because every claimant must wait a year, beginning when his first claim is filed, before new benefit rights can be accumulated based on fresh wage credits.[13]

At least one state[14] actually provides precisely for wiping out all but one week of a claimant's benefit entitlement if the claimant left work voluntarily or refused an offer of work. This clearly was not the result Congress had hoped to accomplish:

> Severe disqualifications, particularly those which cancel (as opposed to postpone) earned monetary entitlement, are not in harmony with the basic purposes of an unemployment insurance system. Most disqualifications under State law provisions are applied for voluntary terminations without good cause (frequently cause must be attributable to an employer), or for refusals of suitable work. Such a situation may represent an error in judgment on the part of the worker, or be the result of circumstances over which he had no control. The penalty for a disqualifying act should not be out of proportion to the disqualifying act.[15]

The National Commission on Unemployment Compensation made only one recommendation to Congress in the area of disqualifications. It went beyond the standard described above and recommended that Congress prohibit not only *total* reduction of benefit rights, but *any* reduction of benefit rights, except for fraud or receipt of disqualifying income.[16] As of early 1983, a dozen states provided for some reduction of benefit rights as the penalty for voluntarily quitting work without good cause and 15 reduced benefit rights of claimants disqualified for refusing suitable work.[17]

Protection Against Automatic Disqualification for Pregnancy

A third standard intended to protect claimants from unreasonable penalties sought elimination of the provisions of 19 states as of the mid-1970s,

> . . . which, in effect, deny benefits because of pregnancy. They vary from State to State, but they are all inequitable in that they deny benefits without regard to the woman's ability to work, availability for work, or efforts to find work. Under eligibility provisions applicable to all claimants, including pregnant women, anyone who is physically unable to work or who is unavailable for work is ineligible for benefits. These determinations are made on the basis of the facts of each individual case and make discriminatory disqualifications because of pregnancy unnecessary.[18]

The standard, enacted in 1976, prohibits benefit denial solely on the basis of pregnancy or termination of pregnancy.

Provisions of the 19 states concerning pregnant women varied considerably in application and severity, ranging from Delaware's disqualification only for any week the individual was actually unable to work because of pregnancy, to Utah's automatic denial of benefits for 12 weeks before the date of childbirth and 6 weeks following childbirth. Ironically, some of the state provisions may have been based on the following Social Security Board's 1942 suggestion for state legislation:

> *Provided further, however,* that a woman shall be considered unable to work for the period within two weeks before the anticipated date of childbirth

and four weeks after childbirth unless it is shown by facts such as a doctor's or midwife's certificate or by her work record during previous periods of pregnancy that she is able to work during such period.[19]

By the time the 1976 standard was enacted, the Utah pregnancy provision had been declared unconstitutional by the U.S. Supreme Court. The Court had ruled that:

> . . . the Utah unemployment compensation statute's incorporation of a conclusive presumption of incapacity during so long a period before and after childbirth is constitutionally invalid. . . .[20]

The adoption of the federal standard, which categorically prohibits denial of benefits solely on the basis of pregnancy or termination of pregnancy, settled any questions that may have remained even after this decision, including the legitimacy of pregnancy provisions that contained rebuttable, rather than conclusive, presumptions of unavailability or inability to work.

In any event, no special provisions dealing with pregnancy now exist in state UI laws. The standard, however, covers only one aspect of sex discrimination found in these laws. A number of states still provide special disqualifications for claimants unemployed because they left work to marry, to accompany their spouses to a new location, or to meet domestic obligations. In most cases, the individual is disqualified for benefits until another job is found, a specified minimum amount is earned, and the individual is then separated for nondisqualifying reasons. Almost invariably women are the victims of these disqualifications.

Dependents' allowance provisions and practices in the dozen or so states that provide these supplements are another example. Such allowances are often granted to male claimants more readily than to female claimants. The latter must usually make a greater effort to prove her children are her dependents.

Women are also disproportionately represented among claimants subject to certain voluntary quit provisions. Most states do not exempt from disqualification claimants who had good personal cause for leaving work. Unless the individual had good cause "attributable to the employer," the disqualification is imposed. This limitation on good cause results in benefit denial for any individual who must leave work to meet a domestic emergency (e.g., to care for a sick child or spouse, to accompany a spouse to another job) or for other compelling personal reasons. The usual reasoning for so limiting good cause to that connected with the work or the employer is that it is not reasonable to expect the employer to bear the costs of unemployment he did not cause. This assumes a necessary linkage between benefit and financing provisions, which experience rating encourages. In any event, for those concerned with eliminating discriminatory provisions, the prohibition of disqualification on the grounds of pregnancy represented a gain, but did not go far enough.[21]

Proposed Benefit Standards

No discussion of federal program standards aimed at protecting claimants would be complete without mention of proposed benefit standards which, though never enacted, have generated more controversy than any other.[22] The controversy arises because standards affecting weekly benefit amounts and the duration of benefits payable pose a greater cost potential than any other type of requirement. Proposed benefit standards sometimes have also covered qualifying requirements and disqualification rules. Four national administrations have fought for benefit standards without success. The states continue to exercise complete authority over these areas, the most important aspects of unemployment insurance. In 1950, President Truman proposed comprehensive UI changes, including minimum benefit standards, as part of a special message to Congress. The bill incorporating the proposed standards did not survive the House Ways and Means Committee. President Eisenhower did not propose benefit standards, but recommended instead that the states seek on their own to meet appropriate benefit adequacy goals. In 1959, a benefit standards bill failed by one vote to clear the Ways and Means Committee. The Kennedy and Johnson Administrations included benefit standards in their UI legislative proposals. The 1965 bills (S. 1991 and H.R. 8282) included the following requirements for states:

(a) a weekly benefit amount equal to at least 50 percent of the claimant's average weekly wage;

(b) a maximum weekly benefit amount equal to at least 66-2/3 of the statewide average weekly wage, to be phased in by July 1, 1971;

(c) a qualifying requirement of not more than 20 weeks of work or the equivalent in earnings during the prior base period;

(d) a maximum of at least 26 weeks duration of weekly benefits payable for claimants meeting such requirement;

(e) a maximum of six weeks suspension of benefits for disqualification for most causes, with no reduction or cancellation of benefit rights.

No state law met all of these proposed requirements and few met any of them at that time. Following hearings in 1966, most of these standards passed the Senate, failed the House, and could not be agreed upon in the House-Senate conference. No UI legislation was adopted because of the impasse.

The Nixon Administration's 1975 UI proposals included a weekly and maximum benefit amount standard similar to (a)

and (b) above. The proposed standards were defeated soundly on the House floor.

In July 1975, a majority of the state agency administrators
comprising the Interstate Conference of Employment Security Agencies supported the same kind of federal benefit
amount standard. Four years later, the same organization
overwhelmingly reversed its position. In 1980, by a 7 to 5
vote, the National Commission on Unemployment Compensation endorsed substantially the same standard, to be phased in gradually by 1986.

Cost is probably the major reason weekly benefit amount
standards have regularly been defeated. The Commission
estimated that the increase in costs in 1980 of setting benefit
ceilings to at least 55 percent of average wages would be
about 15 percent overall; ranging from no increase in states
that already provide a maximum at least that high, to over
100 percent increase in Alaska. If maximums were raised to
60 percent, the national cost would rise by about 19 percent;
and at 66-2/3 percent, it would rise by about 25 percent
above 1979 levels.[23]

A second, less significant, reason for opposition to weekly
benefit amount standards is apprehension that they will lead
to additional standards and ultimately to federalization of
the program. To prevent states from compensating for the
increase in costs caused by higher weekly benefits by tightening qualifying, duration and disqualification provisions,
Congress may consider standardizing *all* benefit provisions,
thereby finally removing all remaining vestiges of state
autonomy. As a further calamity, it is argued that at the
same time Congress eliminates state authority over substantive program matters, it is likely to saddle the states with
responsibility for raising the taxes needed to meet the increased costs.

Most opponents of a weekly benefit amount standard do not contest the need to maintain adequate benefit levels. Most even agree with the minimum 50 percent weekly wage replacement goal. The sticking points are the level of the maximum weekly benefit amounts and, equally important, whether it should be the subject of a federal standard.[24]

Standards that Restrict Payment

If Congress determined at certain times that the states were too harsh on claimants, at other times it focused on state provisions and practices it considered too lenient. In recent years, financial crises and the desire to find ways of reducing costs have produced additional motivations for restrictive federal standards. Whether protective or restrictive, the results of imposing federal standards were the same: a further diminution of state authority; the removal of an issue from the arena of debate; and inequities that invariably follow decisions adopted without adequate consideration. In very few cases has a program standard adopted by Congress been based on careful consideration of available experience at the state level. This is ironic since the federal-state system provides the opportunity for individual states to serve as experimental laboratories. Indeed, the Committee on Economic Security believed that the lack of experience in this country with unemployment insurance,

> . . . clearly suggests the desirability of permitting considerable variation, so that we may learn through demonstration what is best.[25]

The failure to base standards more on state experience may simply reflect the fact that individuals with different values assess experience differently. What is the "best" qualifying requirement from the standpoint of low-wage workers, for example, may be the least desirable from a budget cutter's perspective. This does not detract from the advantages of having individual laboratories or the value of individual state experience to other states, if not to Congress for standard setting purposes. Many program improvements now in most states' laws originated first in single states on an experimental basis.

"Double Dip" Restriction

In 1970 Congress reacted to an apparent loophole in some state benefit formulas that made it possible for claimants to qualify for two successive rounds of benefits without intervening employment. The so-called "double dip" was possible because in many states there is a substantial gap in time between an individual's base period and his benefit year (see footnote 13). In some states, when an individual first files a claim for benefits, he automatically establishes a four-quarter base period in the recent past for the purpose of measuring his work experience. The amount of work performed and the wages paid during the base period determine if he qualifies for benefits and, if so, the weekly benefit amount and the number of weeks of benefits payable. The filing of the claim establishes also the individual's benefit year. This is a one-year period, usually beginning with the date of the first claim, during which he may draw his benefit entitlement.

In most states, the base period is defined as the first four of the last five completed calendar quarters immediately preceding the first claim. These states usually maintain records for every worker showing the wages paid, as reported by employers on a quarterly basis. The gap between the claimant's base period and benefit year eases administration by making it likely that complete information on the claimant's wages is available for the first four of the last five completed calendar quarters. The fifth quarter, or the most recent completed quarter, is called a "lag" quarter. Wage credits earned during the lag quarter and in the following quarter will not be available for benefit purposes until after the claimant finishes his benefit year, files another first claim, and establishes a new benefit year and base period.

For example, a claimant who first filed any time between April 1 and June 30, 1982, would have the four quarters of calendar year 1981 as a base period. The wages earned during the first and second quarters of 1982 would not be counted. However, those "lag" wages would be included in the claimant's next base period if he filed a new claim and established a new benefit year before July 1, 1983.

The "double dip" occurred because some states did not require earnings in more than one quarter, or in much more than one quarter, in order to qualify for benefits. In those states the individual in the example could collect benefits in a second benefit year solely on the basis of those first and second quarter 1982 lag-period wages that were not used before, without having been employed since the beginning of his first benefit year.

The claimant would have to be unemployed in order to establish a new entitlement and meet all the eligibility conditions of the law. Collecting benefits solely on the basis of his lag-period wages could reasonably be considered an abuse on the claimant's part. However, it did constitute an administrative loophole in that it provided more than was probably intended. In 1970 the "double dip" was possible in 15 states. Other states either required substantially more than one quarter of wages to qualify, or some employment subsequent to the start of the first benefit year, or operated without a base period-benefit year lag by requesting recent information on each claimant from the employer when the claim was first filed.

The federal standard requires, as a condition for tax credit, that a state law provide,

. . . an individual who has received compensation during his benefit year is required to have had work since the beginning of such year in order to qualify for compensation in his next benefit year.[26]

Prior to adopting the standard, no effort was made to evaluate the experience of states where the "double dip" was possible—in terms of the work experience of individuals who qualified for it, cost to the state, or any other criteria. It is not clear why this issue was considered sufficiently serious to warrant a federal standard prohibiting anyone from qualifying twice without intervening work—but not serious enough for Congress to bother prescribing precisely how much work should be required. That was left to the states. DOL recommended not more than three weeks of work or the equivalent in wages (e.g., six times the weekly benefit amount), but it provided no reason for choosing this amount.[27] As of 1983, state requirements ranged from amounts equal to from three to ten times the claimant's weekly benefit amount.[28]

Restriction of Benefits
to Certain Aliens

A second restrictive standard was adopted in 1976 as part of a comprehensive unemployment insurance bill. The standard was provoked by the belief of its sponsor, Congressman Sisk of California, that despite illegal aliens being ineligible for UI (because they are not genuinely available for work in this country), many are nevertheless drawing benefits. The standard appears to have been a reaction to abuses of the UI system alleged in a television program. It represented a reaction also to a recent California agency decision to stop asking claimants whether they are citizens or aliens.

The standard requires states to prohibit benefits based on services performed by an alien unless he was lawfully present in the United States either for the purpose of performing such services, or was admitted for permanent residence, or was residing in the U.S. under color of law at the time the services were performed.[29] In discussion of how the standard, which provides no specific penalties, would prevent illegal aliens from drawing benefits, Congressman Sisk advised that,

> . . . really when we get down to it, on the basis that a person might swear to anything in order to get some money if he wants to do it, this statement really becomes a sense-of-Congress statement that we do not believe illegal aliens should draw unemployment compensation.[30]

During the House floor discussion on the standard, no facts and no estimates were offered concerning the number of illegal aliens collecting unemployment benefits.

The standard did generate concern that it might lead to administrative harassment of minority ethnic groups, whether or not they were citizens or otherwise eligible for benefits. This and other concerns were reflected in discussion of amendments to the standard aimed at ensuring that benefits are denied only to aliens not lawfully admitted, without penalizing either citizens or lawfully admitted aliens. Under the amendments, any information required by a state agency to determine a claimant's alien status shall be uniformly required of *all* applicants for benefits, and that no determination denying benefits under the standard shall be made except on a preponderance of the evidence.[31]

In conforming their unemployment insurance laws with the standard, as amended, most states used the same language as the standard.

The Unemployment Insurance Service (UIS) issued instructions advising the states that all claimants should be asked the same *basic* questions on the claims forms as follows:

'Are you a citizen of the U.S.?'
'If "no," when you were working in the U.S., were
you issued an Alien Registration Card, Form I-151,
commonly called a "green card"?'
'If "no," when you were working in the U.S., what
document or form number were you issued?'

To guide staff with regard to the last two questions, the UIS issued almost 30 pages of instructions describing different categories of aliens and the various documents issued to them identifying their status and whether or not they are permitted to work.[32] This was followed by a substantial number of detailed procedural instructions. Neither the Department of Labor nor the states keeps records showing how many, if any, individuals are denied benefits on the basis of the requirements of the standard.

The National Commission on Unemployment Compensation recommended unanimously that the entire standard be eliminated as it was ineffective, unnecessary, and inappropriate as a federal standard. It concluded that the standard would not deter a determined alien from filing for UI, that there is no record of a single individual being denied by reason of the standard, that aliens not legally in the U.S. are ineligible anyway for benefits, and that the provision has unnecessarily burdened the administration of the program and delayed payment of benefits to aliens who are eligible.[33]

Restriction of Benefits to Professional Athletes

Another restrictive federal program standard enacted in 1976 sought to curtail another alleged abuse of the system. As with the standard on aliens, this one was apparently also a reaction to abuses alleged in a television program which included an interview with "a professional golfer who collects unemployment benefits." It was discovered that not only golfers, but also professional ball players apparently were eligible for benefits. According to Congressman Sisk,

> . . . it is a matter of record that regulations of some States make professional athletes eligible for unemployment compensation. It was reported last March, for example, that the president of the Milwaukee Brewers confirmed that some members of the team have been drawing jobless payments for a number of years.[34]

In the House floor discussion of the standard, no facts were presented and no estimates given of the number of professional athletes collecting benefits and the circumstances under which such benefits were paid.

The standard requires states to deny benefits based on any services,

> . . . substantially all of which consist of participating in sports or athletic events or training or preparing to so participate, for any week which commences during the period between two successive sport seasons (or similar periods) and there is a reasonable assurance that such individual will perform such service in the later of such seasons (or similar periods).[35]

The National Commission on Unemployment Compensation unanimously recommended that the standard be eliminated, as unnecessary, discriminatory and difficult to administer. It was unnecessary because athletes on a 12-month contract would not be considered unemployed during the off season. In no state would benefits be permitted if the athlete limits his availability during the off season to participation in his sport. It was discriminatory because it would automatically deny benefits to athletes during the off season (if they have a reasonable assurance of resuming the sport the next season), regardless of whether or not they are available for other kinds of work during the off season.

The standard is difficult to administer because it requires the following special determinations:

1. If "substantially all" the individual's services during the base period were in sports or athletic events;

2. Of the beginning and ending of a "sport season" and the length of the period between successive seasons (which vary among different sports and individuals);

3. If the individuals who performed services as professional athletes in the last season have a reasonable assurance that they will do so in the next season;

4. If the individual performing the services was self-employed or an employer.[36]

As in the case with the standard concerning aliens, there is no record of how many individuals have been denied benefits under the terms of the standard.

The standard restricting the eligibility of athletes, like the standard discussed below prohibiting benefits to school employees between terms, represents an attempt to deal with prominent aspects of the general issue of seasonal unemployment. This issue was first identified by the Committee on Economic Security in reporting that English experience demonstrated that seasonal industries would cause a heavy drain on unemployment funds "unless the benefits to seasonal workers are limited to unemployment occurring within the usual season for that particular industry."[37] However, most states that applied special seasonal restrictions for certain industries or operations or workers encountered administrative problems as difficult as those described above. Moreover, it was never demonstrated that benefits to seasonal workers constituted substantial drains on state UI funds. As of early 1983, fewer than a dozen states had special seasonal provisions, and some of these are rarely applied or applied only with respect to a few specific industries.[38] In most states no distinction is made between seasonal and nonseasonal work or wages in crediting a worker's employment toward meeting the qualifying requirement. Adequate minimum wage and work qualifying requirements have succeeded in automatically screening out individual claimants whose only or primary employment has been in limited seasonal work. Moreover, most states question carefully the availability for work of UI claimants who earned a large part of their base-period wages in seasonal employment, particularly if they are filing for benefits during the off season of the industry in which the wages were earned.[39]

Deduction of Retirement Income from Benefits

There has been less agreement on the question of whether or not retirement income should be deducted from benefits than on most issues.[40] Those who favor reducing a claimant's weekly benefit amount by the prorated weekly amount of his pension argue that no individual should receive duplicate payments for not working. Moreover, if the individual is already receiving a pension, he is not in need of unemployment benefits. They contend that eligibility and receipt of a pension are proof of the recipient's withdrawal from the labor force. They claim also that it is unfair to expect any employer to finance a former worker's pension as well as his unemployment benefits.

Those who oppose deducting pensions from unemployment benefits counter these arguments on the grounds that retirement benefits and unemployment benefits are not duplicate payments, since they are paid for different contingencies. They argue that any presumption that a pension recipient has withdrawn from the labor force should be rebuttable, not conclusive. Moreover, it can be tested by applying regular availability and work search requirements. It may be true that a pension recipient may be in less need than other claimants for unemployment benefits, but the same reasoning could apply to others with nonwage sources of income such as rents or interest. In any event, need is not supposed to be a consideration in determining eligibility. As for the unfair double burden that may fall on employers, they point out that this can apply only to a claimant's base-period employers since only they would be financing both unemployment and pension payments.

Prior to adoption of a federal program standard, the lack of consensus on the desirability and manner of pension deduction was reflected in the variety of state provisions on the issue. Most states provided for reduction of benefits by pension income, but only pensions financed in whole or in larger part by base-period employers. Some deducted all pension income but Social Security, and several provided for no deduction at all. There were variations of each of these provisions.

In 1976 the Senate Finance Committee, in reporting out a bill containing comprehensive unemployment insurance amendments, included a pension deduction standard. The standard would have disqualified from unemployment insurance completely any individual receiving any retirement income regardless of the amount. This severe proposal was amended in its final form, as enacted in 1976, to require each state to simply reduce a claimant's weekly unemployment benefit by the prorated weekly amount of any pension or retirement benefit he receives. Even this standard was more stringent than any existing state provision. Perhaps for that reason, the standard's effective date was postponed to 1979,

> . . . thereby permitting the National Commission on
> Unemployment Compensation an opportunity for

a thorough study of this issue and the Congress to
act in light of its findings and recommendations.[41]

In its first interim report issued November 1978, the Commission recommended unanimously that the pension deduction standard be eliminated. This recommendation was repeated in its July, 1980 Final Report with an additional recommendation that, failing repeal of the standard, Congress move to reduce its severity.

By the time the NCUC Final Report was issued, Congress had already acted, not to abolish the standard, but at least to modify it.[42] The resulting federal standard on pension deduction represents a minimum requirement. States may enact provisions that are more severe, but they may not enact less restrictive pension deductions. As amended, the standard requires states to deduct from the UI benefit the employer-financed portion of a pension contributed to by a UI base-period employer if that employer's contribution affected the claimant's eligibility for or increased the amount of the pension. Social Security Act or Railroad Retirement Act pensions are deductible regardless of the effect of the base-period employer's contribution. The state may, but is not required to, adjust the amount of the pension deduction after taking into account any contributions to the pension made by the employee.[43]

In considering the latter provision, the Senate rejected an amendment proposed by Senator Javits of New York that would require, rather than permit, a state to take into account any and all contributions the individual made to his pension. The amendment was vigorously opposed by the manager of the bill, Senator Boren of Oklahoma, who declared that the Javits amendment was not "based upon a correct observation of what the unemployment insurance system is meant to do." The amendment, he said,

> . . . would allow an abuse of the system by people
> who are not in the work force, who are retired, who
> have decided to retire and draw a pension and
> simply are looking to gain additional unemploy-
> ment benefits on the side when they are no longer
> part of the work force.[44]

After being advised by Senator Bellman that the Javits
amendment would add between $5 and $10 million to the
fiscal year 1980 cost of the unemployment insurance system,
and being urged by that senator to reject the amendment on
those grounds, the Senate voted down the Javits amendment
69 to 23.[45]

The National Commission on Unemployment Compensation considered any federal standard in this area wholly inappropriate, presumptuous and unnecessary in light of the fundamental disagreements among states as to the desirability of
deducting retirement pay from UI and even greater differences concerning the extent to which deductions should
apply.

The standard was clearly not an area where uniformity
was absolutely essential. It was not based on any significant
evaluation of state experience with pension deduction provisions. It had little or no support or input from state agencies.
It reflected three factors that have increasingly influenced
federal decisions on unemployment insurance matters: a
suspicion of unemployed workers who apply for benefits; a
skepticism of the ability of the system to correct abuses; an
overriding concern with the cost implications of program
proposals.

Standards With Both Protective
and Restrictive Features

Two important standards, coverage and extended benefit
standards, cannot be classified solely as either protective or

restrictive. Each is a conglomerate of several related requirements, not all adopted at the same time, and not all reflecting the same motivation.

Coverage Standard

Universal coverage of wage and salary employment has been an unemployment insurance objective since the beginning of the program. Coverage extension has been a gradual process over the years, with some states pioneering in this area but with major advances coming from federal legislation. The latter extensions (employment in small firms, agricultural, and domestic household service) have been accomplished by broadening the applicability of the federal unemployment tax. This was done either by redefining subject "employment" or "employer" to include the new groups, or simply by eliminating prior exclusions. State UI coverage followed, since without coverage by state law and application of the state UI tax, the employers in question would not qualify for credit against the federal tax and their employees would not be protected by unemployment insurance.

Nonprofit and Public Employment

Unlike all other coverage extensions, most employment in nonprofit organizations and in state and local governments was brought into the system by the 1970 and 1976 FUTA amendments making state coverage of these groups a federal standard.[46] Failure of a state to cover a political subdivision or a nonprofit hospital, for example, would threaten the denial of tax credit for *all* covered and taxable employers in the state. Coverage of these categories was accomplished this way to avoid making nonprofit organizations subject to the federal tax[47] and to avoid the constitutional prohibition against imposing a federal tax on states or their subdivisions.[48]

State coverage of nonprofit organizations with four or more employees was mandated by the 1970 amendments to the FUTA. It extended the UI umbrella to about two million nonprofit jobs.[49] The 1970 amendments also extended coverage to some state jobs (those in state hospitals and institutions of higher education) but the bulk of state and local government employment was brought into the system as a result of the comprehensive 1976 amendments to the FUTA. By that time, 29 states had already extended coverage to most state government workers without any federal incentive, but only eight states had covered local government employees on a mandatory basis (some allowed voluntary coverage). The 1976 amendments brought approximately 600,000 jobs in state government and some 7.7 million jobs in local government into the program. There seems little question that coverage of these groups would not have been accomplished to any comparable extent by the states acting alone, in the absence of the 1970 and 1976 federal amendments.

Adoption of the coverage standard for these categories raised two types of issues. The first included broad questions such as the following:

- Does the standard require unqualified state coverage of every category of public employment, or was it enough if a state covered only substantially all employment in a category, such as only those subject to the state merit system?
- Does mandatory state coverage of state and local government workers as a condition for tax credit for other covered employers so intrude the federal government into state budgeting and personnel matters as to violate the Tenth Amendment to the Constitution?
- Does mandated coverage of employment in primary and secondary schools extend to church-related schools, or

do the latter continue to be exempt by reason of certain remaining FUTA exclusions of religious organizations?

These questions were resolved only after conformity hearings or Supreme Court decisions. They are discussed in chapter 5.

The second category of issues related to interpretations of specific exclusions from the otherwise required coverage. These exclusions include services performed in the employ of a church or an organization operated primarily for religious purposes; services performed by a minister or by members of a religious order in the exercise of religious duties; and services performed for a nonprofit organization with fewer than four employees. Permitted exclusions to state and local government coverage, as well as nonprofit organizations, include services performed by employees in the exercise of their duties as: elected officials; members of legislative bodies or the judiciary; members of the State National Guard or the Air National Guard; employees hired for the duration of such emergencies as fire, storm, snow, earthquake, flood; participants in sheltered workshops; inmates of a custodial or penal institution; participants in publicly financed unemployment work-relief or work-training programs; and employees in major nontenured policymaking or advisory positions, or in policymaking or advisory positions requiring eight or fewer hours of work per week.[50]

In addition, services already excluded from the federal act could continue to be excluded even if performed for a nonprofit organization or state or local government. These included service performed by a student for a school in which he is enrolled, service not in the course of the employer's business for which remuneration is less than $50, service for a foreign government or international organization, service performed in the delivery of newspapers by an individual under 18, and others.[51]

Within a short period, issues concerning the scope of the permitted exemptions were resolved. They included, for example, a Kentucky provision excluding temporary employees of the state legislature; refusal by the Idaho legislature to extend coverage to the Boise Symphony Orchestra; an Ohio provision excluding state employees paid on a commission basis; and a proposal at the federal level in 1977[52] to add substitute teachers to the list of exclusions. In each case, the state exemptions were found inconsistent with the federal standard and eventually disapproved. The federal proposal was not enacted.

Questions concerning services already excluded from the federal act focused on the scope of the exclusion of services performed in the employ of a school by a student enrolled and regularly attending classes at the school, and services performed by individuals under the age of 22 who are enrolled in work study programs. Issues arose over the phrase "regularly attending" and its application to doctoral candidates, and proposals to apply the work-study exemption to individuals older than 22. In each case, the Unemployment Insurance Service (UIS) offered interpretations which resolved these and a host of other issues. The UIS issued an 85 page Draft Bill providing draft statutory language for state consideration in implementing the 1976 amendments, commentary and explanatory material and five lengthy and detailed supplements covering a wide range of questions, many of which related to the coverage standard and its implications.[53]

Reimbursement Financing

A significant part of the conglomerate coverage standard concerns the financing of benefits paid to employees of nonprofit organizations and state and local governments. For a number of reasons, these groups of employers were given a special advantage in the form of a financing option other than taxes and experience rating. For many years, the most important obstacle to extending coverage to nonprofit organizations was recognition that since many had very tight budgets and depended on voluntary contributions for financing, they "should not be required to share in the costs of providing benefits to workers in profit-making enterprises."[54] In other words, they should not be forced to finance benefits through taxes which cover not only their own costs but pooled costs as well, including benefit costs charged to but not financed by the employer who is already at the maximum tax rate, costs attributable to employers who go out of business, and noncharged benefit costs.

States that had taken the initiative and already covered their own employees were never forced to be subject to the experience rating standard. That standard required only that reduced rates to "persons" be based on their experience, as measured by the state's system of experience rating. Governments are not "persons" for this purpose.

Accordingly, Congress directed the following preferred treatment for nonprofit organizations and state and local governments:

> . . . the State law shall provide that a governmental entity or any other organization (or group of governmental entities or other organizations) which, but for the requirements of this paragraph, would be liable for contributions with respect to service to which paragraph (1) applies may elect, for such minimum period and at such time as may be provided by State law, to pay (in lieu of such contributions) into the State unemployment fund amounts equal to the amounts of compensation attributable under the State law to such service. The State law may provide safeguards to ensure that governmental entities or other organizations so

electing will make the payments required under such elections.[55]

The requirement, that states offer governmental entities and nonprofit organizations the reimbursement option, generated more issues than did the provisions requiring coverage of these employers. Since they paid no federal tax, the administrative costs attributable to their workers (and the federal share of extended benefits paid to their former employees in the case of nonprofit organizations) are absorbed by private sector employers. The major issue was the extent, if any, states could shift still other costs to the private sector by not charging reimbursing employers for certain benefits. This issue was the subject of a conformity hearing and is treated in chapter 5.

Most other reimbursement issues were resolved soon after issuance of Department guidelines. Early issues arose over a proposed amendment in one state to set the effective period for an election to reimburse or contribute at no less than ten years; another state proposal to require any employer wishing to elect the reimbursement method to post a bond equal to $50,000; a proposed amendment to limit the reimbursement option only to the state as a whole and not to its component units; a proposed state regulation requiring deposit of reimbursements in special state funds; a bill to allow employers with a positive experience rating balance to apply that balance to offset future liability incurred as a reimburser; and another to prohibit employers whose experience rating accounts showed that their benefit charges exceeded their contributions from electing the reimbursement option. All these provisions were reviewed by DOL and considered inconsistent with the reimbursement standard.

The reimbursement option is likely to continue to be a source of friction, particularly during high cost and high tax periods. Yet, this sole departure from experience rating in 35 years helped make possible the coverage of nonprofit organizations and governmental entities by overcoming arguments that coverage would be inequitable since the taxes collected would far exceed the benefit costs of these traditionally low turnover employing units.

Equal Treatment Requirement

In extending coverage to jobs in nonprofit organizations and state and local government, Congress apparently anticipated that states might adopt measures to cut costs that would undermine the intent of extending protection to workers in these jobs on the same basis as others. For example, states conceivably could establish special qualifying requirements, a separate benefit structure, or separate eligibility conditions applicable only to public and nonprofit employees. For a number of reasons, states might be more likely to single out public employees for restrictive treatment than other workers. Each state is directly liable for financing the benefit costs of its own employees, and it might be subject to substantial pressure from political subdivisions for relief from benefit costs they incur. Pressure for cutting public employee benefit costs might also ensue from taxpayer groups as well as competing interests for public funds. In the case of nonprofit organizations, their employees might be the subject of special treatment as a reaction to their employers' immunity from federal tax and the advantage they enjoy of electing to finance benefit costs on a reimbursement instead of a state tax basis.

Some evidence existed that states might discriminate against certain employees. A 1960 federal amendment[56] allowed states to extend coverage to services performed on American ships under certain conditions. Although the law provided that these maritime employees be treated the same as other workers, no penalty for violation was included. Ohio enacted special restrictive requirements relating to Great Lakes seamen. Consequently, the 1970 federal law amendments included a special provision denying maritime employers credit against the federal tax if a state does not treat their employees on an equal basis with other workers.[57]

Regardless of whether or not such Congressional apprehensions either existed (relevant Congressional reports provide no explanation) or were realistic, the result was enactment of an "equal treatment" standard requiring all states to provide compensation to employees of nonprofit organizations and state and local government employees,

> . . . in the same amount, on the same terms, and subject to the same conditions as compensation . . . payable on the basis of other service subject to the State Law.[58]

School Employees: Between-Terms Denial Requirements

The extension of coverage to nonprofit organizations and state and local government workers in 1970 and 1976 was not an unqualified blanket protection of all such workers. Most school employees did not perform services for the school during the break between terms. They were not considered by Congress to be "unemployed" then, within the meaning of unemployment insurance, particularly if they were assured of reemployment with the school the second term and certainly if they were employed under 12-month contracts. It is not clear how this category of workers is distinguishable from other groups of workers similarly circumstanced. Automobile workers are regularly laid off on a temporary basis during recurring model change-over periods. Longshoremen, fishermen, farm workers and many other occupations are no less seasonal than school employees.

School workers are large in numbers, often well organized, relatively well paid and usually regularly employed. But the main distinguishing feature is that most are public employees, subject to public criticism and tight budgetary restraints. Most, particularly teachers, were generally considered fortunate to enjoy a lengthy "vacation" each year and indeed this was probably a strong motivation of some for entering the profession. The prospect of paying benefits to these workers during school breaks was considered neither consistent with unemployment insurance objectives nor desirable from the standpoint of fund solvency. Congress was skeptical that the states' availability and work search requirements could limit benefits to the few teachers genuinely ready, willing and able to work during the school break. Evidently, Congress was distrustful even of the states' willingness or ability to enact appropriate restrictions.

The special protection afforded nonprofit and public employees by reason of the equal treatment requirement was, therefore, counterbalanced by a standard providing a special disqualification applicable to school employees:

> . . . with respect to services in an instructional, research, or principal administrative capacity for an educational institution . . . , compensation shall not be payable based on such services for any week commencing during the period between two successive academic years or terms (or, when an agreement provides instead for a similar period between two regular but not successive terms, during such period) to any individual if such individual performs such services in the first of such academic years (or terms) and if there is a contract or reasonable assurance that such individual will perform services in any such capacity for any educational institution in the second of such academic years or terms.[59]

The above paragraph requires the denial of benefits to "professional" employees of schools (instructors, researchers, principal administrators) during the periods between school terms if they worked for the school during the first term and have a contract or a reasonable assurance of work for the school during the next term in the same or another professional capacity. States were given the option to extend the between-terms denial to nonprofessional employees (e.g., bus drivers, cafeteria workers, school crossing guards) of schools below the college level, but not to nonprofessional employees of colleges and universities. Apparently the latter were not made subject to any between-terms requirement because the thinking in 1970 (when they were first covered) was that they were less likely than professionals to have 12-month contracts, and in addition their jobs were not really different from their counterparts in private industry. They remained untouched by extension of the restrictive provisions in 1976, apparently on the grounds that once the conditions of their coverage had been established, it would be unfair to subject them to new restrictions. This anomalous result was corrected in 1982 by an amendment requiring states that choose the option to deny benefits to nonprofessional employees of primary and secondary schools to include in the denial nonprofessional employees of colleges and universities. In other words, nonprofessional employees of all educational institutions in a state must now be treated alike.[60]

Most states had adopted the option relating to nonprofessional employees of primary and high schools. Subsequent legislation enacted in 1977 permitted states to extend the blanket denial not only during periods between school terms but also during established vacation or holiday periods occurring within terms.[61] Over half the states have adopted this option. Further permission was given, also in 1977, to states to apply the between-terms denial provisions not only to school employees, but also to employees of educational service agencies, defined as governmental agencies or entities established and operated exclusively to provide services for schools.⁶² Few states adopted this option. This is the only extension of the denial provisions to individuals other than school employees.

The between-terms denial requirements have generated more controversy than most standards. They have necessitated a large variety of federal interpretations, including definitions of "educational institutions," "reasonable assurance," "principal administrative capacity," and "term." For example, they presented such questions as: Whether the denial applies to a school principal who has reasonable assurance only for a teacher's job for the coming term; if the denial applies when reasonable assurance of reemployment is conditioned upon community approval of a budget; if the denial applies if reasonable assurance is given but the individual's union has not yet signed a contract; if reasonable assurance is valid when it is provided 200 former employees but budget cuts permit only 150 jobs to be filled during the next term; what assurance of reemployment is appropriate in the case of substitute teachers who worked less than full time the preceding term; if the between-terms requirement is satisfied if an individual, provided reasonable assurance, finds that there is actually no job available during the succeeding term and is then paid benefits retroactively for the summer; if the between-terms denial may apply to school crossing guards employed by governmental entities other than schools. The last two questions were the subjects of conformity hearings, discussed in chapter 5. The question concerning retroactive payment for the summer was finally resolved by a 1982 amendment requiring that nonprofessionals denied benefits between terms and not offered a job for the second term shall be entitled to a retroactive payment, provided they had continued to file claims during the between-terms period.⁶³

The National Commission on Unemployment Compensation found the between-terms denial requirement not an appropriate federal standard. According to the Commission, it reflects a wholly unwarranted Congressional apprehension that, absent the standard, the states would otherwise pay benefits during the summer indiscriminately to school employees who do not really want jobs. However, the action of the great majority of states, in adopting the option to extend the denial to nonprofessional employees of primary and secondary schools, demonstrates that states will indeed act to prevent benefit payments to school employees during school breaks. A divided Commission (8-4) recommended removing all federal between-terms denial requirements, limiting the equal treatment requirement to periods *other* than school breaks, and thus allowing the states to handle between-terms issues as they see fit under the state law.[64]

Extended Benefit Standard

One of the most significant federal program standards was first enacted in 1970.[65] It requires states to provide additional weeks of benefits during heavy periods of unemployment for individuals who exhausted their regular entitlement. Unemployment insurance was intended to tide workers over a temporary period of unemployment. Over the years this objective was translated to mean that enough weeks of benefits should be provided to see the great majority of beneficiaries through their entire spell of unemployment. The average potential duration provided by the states of about 24 weeks seemed adequate in good times when, nationally, only about 20 percent of those filing first claims exhausted their benefits (i.e., drew all their entitlement before finding a job). It was not adequate during recessions, when the exhaustion rate rose to 30 percent or more. Such were the circumstances in the late 1950s by which time most state duration provisions allowed benefits up to a maximum of 26 weeks.

A number of states tried to resolve the issue by raising their regular duration maximum beyond the usual 26 weeks. Other states adopted provisions for temporary extensions of benefits, triggered on only during periods of high unemployment. The federal government approached the problem in the recessions of 1958 and 1961 by enacting temporary programs of extended benefits. The first, the Temporary Unemployment Compensation Act (TUC), provided for voluntary participation by the states and was financed at first by U.S. Treasury advances eventually repaid by state funds. The second, the Temporary Extended Unemployment Compensation Act (TEUC), was financed by FUTA revenues with mandatory participation by all states. Both programs extended benefit duration by 50 percent with an overall maximum of 39 weeks in the second program.[66]

Enactment of a permanent program of extended benefits in 1970 reflected a Congressional conclusion that unemployment during recessions was a joint federal-state responsibility, to be met by state standby programs of extended benefits payable during high unemployment periods and financed on a 50-50 federal-state basis. The extended benefit (EB) program answered long-standing questions of how much of an increase in benefit duration should be provided (an overall limit of 39 weeks was adopted for regular and extended benefits); whether the same number of weeks of EB should be paid to all claimants, or whether EB entitlement should relate directly to regular benefit entitlement (the latter course was chosen); at what level of unemployment EB should become payable (state and national triggering indicators based on insured unemployment rates were specified); whether EB should be voluntary or mandatory (it is mandatory); whether EB claimants should be subject to additional eligibility requirements beyond those required of regular benefit claimants (no added requirement was specified in the 1970 law).

As demonstrated by the 1971 and 1974-76 recession experiences, EB did not obviate the occasional resort to additional federally mandated emergency benefits.[67] The 1970 EB law did, however, effectively relieve the states of any further pressures to provide their own protection beyond the 26th week of unemployment, at least under recession conditions.

Enactment of the EB program represented a major federal intrusion into a substantive program area (duration of benefits) that had (with the brief exceptions of TUC and TEUC) long been the exclusive jurisdiction of the states. However, the extended benefits program was not entirely dominated by the federal partner. Generally, the same eligibility and disqualification provisions that applied to regular claimants applied also to EB claimants. Qualifying requirements and weekly benefit amounts were determined by applying state regular benefit provisions. States thus retained control of these aspects of extended benefits.

Beginning in 1980, however, federal authority expanded even more over the extended benefits area. In the process of developing the fiscal 1981 and subsequent federal budgets, the Administration and Congress sought ways to reduce nondefense spending. In the UI area these proposals took the form of restrictions on the extended benefits program. There have always been many advocates of such restrictions in any case. The budget imperatives of this period helped increase these numbers.

Beginning with the recession of the mid-1970s, the federal and many state unemployment insurance funds were in difficulty. After 1978, liabilities mounted year by year because of unremittingly heavy unemployment. By early 1983 over 20 states had outstanding loans from the federal loan fund amounting to more than $10 billion. More states were expected to borrow in 1983. These deficits provided a negative climate at both state and federal levels for any amendments that would result in increased costs, and an ideal climate for virtually any cost-cutting measure. Pressure to cut benefit costs increased at the state level as unemployment rates continued to climb, deficits increased, and federal amendments were adopted to require interest on moneys borrowed by states from the loan fund.

Most of the restrictive amendments to the EB provisions of the federal UI statute were included in the Omnibus Budget Reconciliation Acts of 1980 and 1981. The first three of those summarized below were estimated to reduce federal program costs in fiscal year 1981 by about $150 million.[68]

Waiting Week

Three of the amendments to extended benefit provisions represented reversals of long-standing federal policy expressed in DOL policy statements and recommendations to the states. The first was intended to provide an incentive for all states to require that claimants serve an uncompensated week of unemployment before they may become eligible for benefits. It provides for elimination of the federal 50 percent matching share for the first week of extended benefits in any state which does not have a waiting period for regular benefits. This applies to states with no waiting week provisions (11 as of October 1981); to states which have a waiting week for which the individual is later reimbursed if still unemployed after a specified period (7); to states whose laws authorize the suspension of the waiting week under emergency conditions (1); and even to states that waive a waiting week requirement if it would interrupt a continuous period of unemployment (5). The amendment affected 24 states in all.

Since 1950, DOL had recommended that states consider eliminating their waiting week requirement.[69] It no longer serves an administrative need, the chief original argument for a waiting period, and it causes a serious delay in providing claimants (many of whom delay filing claims to begin with) with needed income in the early stages of their unemployment. Even in a state meeting the prompt payment standards, payment of the first benefit check will occur no earlier than three full weeks following the first claim, and it will represent compensation for no more than one week of unemployment. Elimination of the waiting week does not shorten the time it takes to process a claim, but the first check covers two weeks of unemployment.

The main argument to eliminate the federal 50 percent matching share for the first week of EB in any state that has no waiting week for regular benefits was that it would save an estimated $25 million in federal costs in fiscal year 1981. The cost savings argument is the most persuasive. There is no question that elimination of the waiting week is a relatively expensive step. In addition, a waiting week requirement represents less of a burden on claimants than most alternative means of cutting comparable amounts of benefit costs. Most unemployed workers have enough resources to get by a payless week at the outset of their unemployment. Moreover, if a claimant remains unemployed and exhausts his benefit entitlement, he will have collected his full entitlement regardless of the waiting week.

A less persuasive argument advanced by supporters of the amendment, is that restoration of the waiting week would induce unemployed workers to look for work rather than "beat a hasty track to the government office":

> If the State wants to go ahead and do away with the 1-week period, if they want to follow the policy of saying that a person has no responsibility to even try to seek employment before drawing the benefits, that would be left to the States. But the Federal taxpayers, including the taxpayers of those States which have already put their own houses in order, should not be asked to fund such a program.

Mr. President, I would suggest that it is certainly not too much to ask that a person try to find work for just 1 week before he turns to the Government and asks for unemployment benefits.[70]

It is not clear how the waiting period would cause unemployed workers to forego filing claims temporarily and begin earnest work searches, since with or without a waiting period, a delay in filing a claim means a delay in benefits. As one Senator observed:

There is no evidence that a 1-week waiting period provides any incentive to find work, rather it only creates an additional hardship for a worker who has lost a job.[71]

Unless he has first filed a claim and thereafter certifies, with respect to such week, that he was able and available for work and seeking work, no individual can receive credit for either a waiting week or a compensable week of unemployment. This is one reason why DOL has consistently recommended that individuals file claims as soon as they are separated. The other reason is to ensure that individuals have exposure as soon as possible to job finding, training, and other assistance available through the employment service.

Disqualification for Duration of the Unemployment

The second amendment that reversed a prior federal position requires all states to provide that extended benefit claimants who were disqualified from regular benefits for a voluntary quit, discharge for misconduct, or refusal of suitable work, meet a subsequent work requirement before they can qualify for extended benefits. Most states have moved to this type of disqualification over the years but some still apply a specific period of benefit suspension after which regular benefits can be paid. This rework or duration type of disqualification is particularly harsh as an extended benefit requirement since it is during periods when EB is payable that jobs are likely to be particularly scarce. It had been consistently opposed for state provisions in the past by the Department of Labor. The disqualification also creates inequities. Claimants whose skills are in demand will be able to meet the requalifying requirement easier than others. Moreover, the disqualification is harder on claimants seeking permanent, full-time work than on claimants looking only for temporary jobs.

The most serious inequity will occur in those states which prescribe a voluntary quit and misconduct disqualification for regular benefits which is different from the disqualification imposed for extended benefits. Claimants who have already satisfied a suspension disqualification may find themselves ineligible for EB because of the same separation that provoked the first disqualification. For this reason, and because of the administrative burden of determining if all EB claimants have had some work since any disqualifying separation, some states with a suspension disqualification for regular benefits have subsequently enacted the more severe duration of the unemployment type of disqualification for regular benefits simply to provide uniform treatment and avoid administrative difficulties. The trend was in that direction before; the new requirement has accelerated it.

Suitable Work and Work Search

The third amendment that reverses federal policy required all states to add special suitable work and work search provisions applicable to extended benefit claimants. Except for individuals whose prospects for work in their usual occupation within a reasonably short period are good, suitable work for an extended benefit claimant is defined as any work within the individual's capabilities that pays at least the higher of the minimum wage or the individual's average weekly benefit amount, and is otherwise suitable within the meaning of state law, disregarding state criteria concerning consistency with the individual's prior training, education, work experience and wage level. All extended benefit claimants must engage in a systematic and sustained effort to obtain work and must provide tangible evidence of that effort. Claimants who fail to meet these requirements must be disqualified for the duration of their unemployment and may become eligible only if they have been subsequently employed for at least four weeks after the disqualification and earned wages equal to at least four times their weekly benefit amount.

This suitable work definition differs substantially from the definition first recommended by the Social Security Board and later in DOL draft bills:

> In determining whether or not any work is suitable for an individual, the (State) Commission should consider the degree of risk involved to his health, safety, and morals, his physical fitness and prior training and experience, his length of unemployment and prospects for securing work in his customary occupation and the distance of the available work from his residence.[72]

This definition reflects the premise that suitable work should vary with the circumstances of each claimant, and the assumption that if a skilled worker is required to accept a job far below his level of skills, the individual is not likely to be there long and, meanwhile, the job is closed to those for whom it really is suitable work. All states already require claimants to lower their sights in terms of the kind of work and level of wages they will accept, as the period of their unemployment lengthens. The new suitable work requirements applicable for EB limit the flexibility of both claimants and state agencies by requiring that the claimant's prior experience and wage levels be eliminated from consideration in determining if a given job offer constitutes suitable work for EB claimants.

Conformity with the new provisions would oblige most states to have one definition of suitable work for regular claimants and another for EB. As observed by one Senator:

> Many States may prefer to avoid that confusion, and if the Congress enacts this provision, the only route open to them would be apply this unfair Federal rule to the regular State program as well.[73]

As for requiring "tangible evidence" of a claimant's efforts to obtain work, DOL recommended against such a provision in the past:

> Proof that a claimant has actively sought work may be an empty gesture, demoralizing to the claimant and a nuisance to employers when no work is available in an area. Such proof should not be required of all claimants by statute. While claimants should be active candidates for jobs as a condition for receiving benefits, the test of availability should be realistic, taking into consideration such factors as business conditions, the penetration of the employment service, the hiring methods in the industry in which the claimant is seeking work and the claimant's individual circumstances.[74]

In advocating the new suitable work provisions for EB, no attempt was made to distinguish between them and the conventional provisions of most state laws which were patterned after the DOL draft bill recommendation.

Since the suitable work requirements for EB were made conditions for credit against the federal tax, at stake for a state considering not to adopt the requirements was not simply denial of the 50 percent federal share of EB but forfeiture also of tax credit for all the state's employers and of all administrative grants.

These three requirements were estimated to reduce federal program costs by $25 million, $32 million and $94 million, respectively, in fiscal year 1981. The appeal for their enactment was made largely, but not only, on that basis. The argument that the claimants affected were long term unemployed and, therefore, lacking in initiative, and the fact that federal funds are used to finance 50 percent of extended benefits were added as justification for the amendments.

Triggers

In 1981 Congress adopted additional restrictive amendments to the EB program. Three involved the criteria for triggering on and off the availability of extended benefits in a state. The first amendment eliminated the national trigger. Prior to the amendment, extended benefits in a state could be made available either by high levels of insured unemployment in the state activating a state trigger, or by a national seasonally adjusted insured unemployment rate of 4.5 percent or more over a 13-week period. The objective of the national triggering of EB was to help limit the impact of a nationwide business downturn. Another argument was that EB meets the needs of the long term unemployed in states with low insured unemployment rates.

In urging elimination of the national trigger, the Administration advanced two arguments: first, that the result would be to target extended benefits only to those states whose workers genuinely need such extra help and thereby save money; and second,

> In addition, I submit that the present system works as a disincentive for the unemployed to become quickly reemployed in those States with low unemployment when the national trigger is on.[75]

The second 1981 trigger amendment increased the level of insured unemployment necessary to activate the state trigger.

Prior to the amendment, extended benefits became payable when a state's insured unemployment rate (IUR) averaged 4 percent or more for 13 weeks and was at least 120 percent of the average IUR for the corresponding 13-week periods in the two preceding years. A state could opt to disregard the 120 percent requirement and trigger on if its current 13-week rate was as much as 5 percent. The 1981 amendments increased from 4 percent to 5 percent the required state IUR trigger level and from 5 percent to 6 percent the optional trigger level for states choosing to waive the 120 percent requirement.

In recommending adoption of the higher trigger points, the Administration argued that "structural changes in the labor force have contributed to a generally higher level of normal unemployment," and that

> The new laws for extended benefits will better reflect these changes and provide these additional benefits where they are truly needed.[76]

The third 1981 trigger change altered the method of calculating the insured unemployment rate (IUR). Prior to the change, the IUR calculation included individuals filing claims for extended benefits as well as regular benefit claimants. The amendment eliminated extended benefit claimants from the count. The Administration's explanation for the change was, in part, that the prior method was "technically flawed and produces several anomalies."[77]

Qualifying Requirement

The final EB standard adopted in 1981 prohibited states from granting federally shared extended benefits to any claimant with fewer than 20 weeks of work, or an equivalent earnings pattern, in his base period. In states that do not use weeks of work as the qualifying requirement, the equivalent to 20 weeks would be total base-period earnings of one and one-half times the claimant's highest quarter of wages, or 40 times the claimant's weekly benefit amount. This amendment was consistent with the 1980 pattern of using EB amendments as leverage for accomplishing changes in states' regular benefit programs. Of course, the amendment also helped cut costs since some claimants did qualify for regular benefits in many states with limited employment or earnings.

According to the Administration, the advantage of the amendment was that it would prevent EB being paid to workers who were employed for less than 20 weeks in the base period.

> Extended unemployment benefits are paid generally from the 27th up to the 39th week of unemployment. Such long-term benefits should not be paid to workers who were employed for less than 20 weeks in the base period. . . .[78]

Actually, extended benefits may be paid to some claimants for weeks of unemployment coming much earlier—as soon as the fourth or fifth week in a few cases—since EB is payable to claimants after they exhaust their regular benefit entitlement which could be much less than 26 weeks. In many states, claimants with less than 39 weeks of base-period work would qualify for fewer than 26 weeks of benefits, and those who worked less than 20 weeks would usually be eligible for less than 15 weeks of regular benefits plus only a few weeks of EB.

The impact of the 1981 EB changes on unemployed workers was substantial, mostly because of changes affecting the triggers. These changes resulted in the payment of extended benefits in many states and in much lower EB outlays overall during the recession year of 1982. On the basis of DOL estimates, outlays for extended benefits that were expected to amount to $4.9 billion in fiscal 1983 under the old law were cut to $1.2 billion as a result of the changes. In fiscal 1984, EB outlays had been estimated at $3.3 billion, but the changes reduced that total to $302 million.

> Put another way, 3.3 million people who would have been eligible for the 13-week extended benefits in fiscal 1983 will not be eligible. Another 2.6 million will be excluded in fiscal 1984 and about 600,000 in fiscal 1985.[79]

Despite the restrictions, the severe unemployment problems of the 1982 recession nevertheless resulted in the establishment of another temporary post-EB program, as occurred in the mid-1970s, although more limited. Congress enacted, with Reagan Administration agreement, a special 6-month program of emergency benefits, wholly federally financed out of general revenue, to become available from September 12, 1982 through March 31, 1983. An individual in a state already triggered on could qualify for a maximum of 10 weeks of "federal supplemental compensation." Eight weeks were available in states not triggered on, but with IURs of at least 3.5 percent. Up to six weeks were available in all other states, regardless of the level of unemployment.[80] The program was expected to cost about $2.1 billion and help about two million workers, thereby temporarily restoring part but not all of the reductions made by the 1981 amendments.[81] The 1981 amendments remained untouched.

Aside from the pressures of an election year, it is not clear how the 1982 rationale for making emergency extended benefits available in states with IURs of less than 5 percent could be reconciled with the 1981 decision to eliminate the federal trigger in the regular EB program and to raise the state "on" triggers from 4 to 5 percent. As it turns out, the only advantage that seems to have resulted from the EB trigger changes with respect to the 1982-1983 period has been a financial one from the point of view of state UI funds and employers, in that federal general revenues replaced UI tax financing for some of the long term benefit protection provided.

Rounding

One additional EB standard was enacted in 1982.[82] It provides a condition (in addition to the waiting week requirement) of state entitlement to the federal 50 percent share of EB costs: if a state does not provide for a benefit formula under which regular benefits are rounded down to the next lower multiple of one dollar, the state will not be entitled to the federal 50 percent matching share on the amount by which extended benefits exceed the amount that would have resulted from such rounding down. The rounding applies to weekly regular benefits, weekly extended benefits, state minimum and maximum weekly benefit amounts, partial benefit payments, amounts payable after deduction for pensions or after any other deductions.

Most states (if not all) currently round uneven benefit amounts to the next higher whole dollar. Although the amendment was expected to save $10 million and $19 million in fiscal years 1984 and 1985, respectively, it is not clear how the excess resulting from current practices will be calculated or how the standard will be enforced in states that do not adopt this requirement.[83] As of early 1983, fewer than a dozen states had adopted the rounding-down requirement.

The extended benefit standards of 1980, 1981 and 1982 were adopted despite the objections of those who questioned the wisdom of making permanent substantive changes ". . . on a piecemeal basis prompted by a sudden fever to cut the budget."[84] Nor were arguments effective that appealed against the provisions from the perspective of the unemployed:

> This is an attempt to change the system which aids
> the unfortunate, and once again, it is the unfor-

tunate without jobs who will suffer. When job
prospects are so poor, why are we trying to lessen
the support of the unemployed? We are doing this
as a cost saving measure, but indirectly we are asking those who can least afford it to pay.[85]

The issue of federal-state relations was raised only briefly:

. . . these amendments allow increased Federal encroachment into a program functioning quite well
at the State level.[86]

—without effect.

These standards are clearly not absolutely essential to the
program. They are not based on states' experience or any
particular problem then confronting the system. They reflect
not only the overriding motivation to cut costs but also the
same distrust of the unemployed and skepticism of the
system's ability to prevent abuses that are characteristic of
most recent federal program standards.

The extended benefit standards are highly significant for
several reasons. They preempt the issue of long term
unemployment for federal determination. They affect more
workers than any of the other standards. By adopting
amendments that reversed long time federal recommendations, almost solely on cost savings grounds, Congress broke
precedent with a 45-year practice of enacting legislation at
least intended to enhance the program's objectives and effectiveness. Through this legislation, Congress seemed to communicate four messages to the states. First, federal responsibility for maintaining a strong and balanced federal-state
partnership is secondary to budget considerations. Second,
as long as "federal funds" are involved, Congress is justified
in imposing its will, notwithstanding traditional state areas
of authority. Third, past federal recommendations in the
program area are not to be considered immutable. Fourth,
additional federal standards are likely to follow unless more

states take steps to "improve" their programs to reflect prevailing federal attitudes toward workers who file for unemployment insurance.

NOTES

1. Section 3304(a)(9)(B), FUTA.

2. U.S. Department of Labor, Manpower Administration, Field Memorandum No. 165-72, *Proposals for Amendments to State Unemployment Insurance Laws or for Regulations to Implement Those Laws,* April 20, 1972.

3. Section 3304(a)(9)(A), FUTA.

4. *Employment Security Amendments of 1969,* Report No. 91-612, Committee on Ways and Means, House of Representatives, 91st Congress, 1st Sess. (November 10, 1969), p. 17.

5. The U.S. and Canada have reciprocal agreements to handle UI claims. Canada serves as agent for individuals who earned their wage credits in a state and file in Canada. Individual states serve as agents for Canada in the case of workers who were employed in Canada and file in a state.

6. P.L. 96-364.

7. Section 3304(a)(8), FUTA.

8. *Employment Security Amendments of 1970,* Report No. 91-752, Committee on Finance, United States Senate, 91st Congress, 2d Sess. (March 26, 1970), p. 22.

9. U.S. Department of Labor, Manpower Administration, *Draft Legislation to Implement the Employment Security Amendments of 1970—H.R. 14705* (1970), p. 62.

10. U.S. Department of Labor, Bureau of Employment Security, Unemployment Compensation Program Letter, No. 78, December 29, 1944.

11. Section 3304(a)(10), FUTA.

12. *Employment Security Amendments of 1970, op. cit.,* p. 23.

13. Under all state laws a claimant is assigned a 12-month benefit year within which he may draw his entitlement based on his preceding 12-month base period. If he exhausts his entitlement before 12 months, he must wait until the expiration of the benefit year, then he may set up a new base period and benefit year, if he has enough qualifying wage credits in the new base period.

14. Colorado. See U.S. Department of Labor, Manpower Administration, *Comparison of State Unemployment Insurance Laws* (Washington, DC), Table 401.

15. *Employment Security Amendments of 1970, op. cit.,* p. 24.

16. *Unemployment Compensation: Final Report* (National Commission on Unemployment Compensation, July 1980), p. 48.

17. *Comparison of State Unemployment Insurance Laws, op. cit.,* Tables 401 and 404.

18. *Unemployment Compensation Amendments of 1975,* Report No. 94-755, Committee on Ways and Means, House of Representatives, 94th Congress 1st Sess. (December 16, 1975), p. 50.

19. Federal Security Agency, Social Security Board, Bureau of Employment Security, *Manual of State Employment Security Legislation, Employment Security Memorandum No. 13* (Revised November 1942), p. 403.

20. *Mary Ann Turner* v. *Department of Employment Security and Board of Review of the Industrial Commission of Utah,* No. 74-1312 (November 17, 1975).

21. *Unemployment Compensation: Final Report, op. cit.,* pp. 174-177.

22. See discussion of proposals made up to 1965 in William Haber and Merrill G. Murray, *Unemployment Insurance in the American Economy* (Homewood, IL: Richard D. Irwin, Inc., 1966), pp. 441-443; later proposals discussed in *Unemployment Compensation: Final Report, op. cit.,* pp. 39-40.

23. *Unemployment Compensation: Final Report, op. cit.,* pp. 40, 41.

24. *Ibid.,* p. 191.

25. Committee on Economic Security, *op. cit.,* p. 15.

26. Section 3304(a)(7), FUTA.

27. U.S. Department of Labor, Manpower Administration, *Draft Legislation to Implement the Employment Security Amendments of 1970—H.R. 14705,* pp. 48-49.

28. *Comparison of State Unemployment Insurance Laws, op. cit.,* Table 302.

29. Section 3304(a)(14), FUTA.

30. *Congressional Record,* July 20, 1976, p. H 7422.

31. *Congressional Record,* September 29, 1976, p. S 17025.

32. U.S. Department of Labor, Employment and Training Administration, *Draft Language and Commentary to Implement the Unemployment Compensation Amendments of 1976—P.L. 94-566* (Supplement #3, Questions and Answers, May 6, 1977).

33. *Unemployment Compensation: Final Report, op. cit.,* p. 33.

34. *Congressional Record,* July 20, 1976, p. H 7421.

35. Section 3304(a)(13), FUTA.

36. *Unemployment Compensation: Final Report, op. cit.,* p. 30.

37. Committee on Economic Security, *op. cit.,* p. 21.

38. *Comparison of State Unemployment Insurance Laws, op. cit.,* p. 3-17.

39. See Merrill G. Murray, *The Treatment of Seasonal Unemployment Under Unemployment Insurance* (Kalamazoo, MI: W. E. Upjohn Institute for Employment Research, April 1972).

40. However, in contrast to the lack of information available in connection with the standards concerning aliens and professional athletes, some studies were available concerning the extent of the alleged problems represented by UI claimants who are drawing pensions. See, for example, Merrill G. Murray, *Should Pensioners Receive Unemployment Compensation?* (Kalamazoo, MI: W. E. Upjohn Institute for Employment Research, August 1967).

41. *Conference Report* (To Accompany H.R. 10210) The Unemployment Compensation Amendments of 1976, Report No. 94-1745, 94th Congress 2d Sess. (October 1, 1976), p. 16.

42. Public Law 96-364, approved September 26, 1980.

43. Section 3304(a)(15), FUTA.

44. *Congressional Record* (March 4, 1980), pp. S 2104-2105.

45. *Ibid.*

46. Section 3304(a)(6)(A), FUTA.

47. *Employment Security Amendments of 1969, op. cit.,* p. 11. Congress was reluctant to extend the federal tax to nonprofit organizations which

must frequently rely on donations and charitable contributions to survive.

48. *Unemployment Compensation Amendments of 1975, op. cit.,* p. 42.

49. *Employment Security Amendments of 1969, op. cit.,* p. 13.

50. Section 3309(b) and (c), FUTA.

51. Section 3306(c), FUTA.

52. H.R. 25620. The bill would have prohibited the payment of benefits at any time based on service as a substitute teacher if the individual was paid on a per diem basis and was employed fewer than 45 days in the base period.

53. U.S. Department of Labor, Employment and Training Administration, *Draft Language and Commentary to Implement the Unemployment Compensation Amendments of 1976—P.L. 94-566.*

54. *Employment Security Amendments of 1970, op. cit.,* p. 14.

55. Section 3309(a)(2), FUTA.

56. P.L. 86-778.

57. P.L. 91-373.

58. Section 3304(a)(6)(A), FUTA.

59. *Ibid.*

60. P.L. 97-248.

61. P.L. 95-19.

62. P.L. 95-171.

63. P.L. 97-248.

64. *Unemployment Compensation: Final Report, op. cit.,* pp. 32, 33.

65. Federal-State Extended Unemployment Compensation Act of 1970.

66. For a discussion of these and the subsequent extended benefits program, see *Unemployment Compensation: Final Report, op. cit.,* pp. 58-69.

67. *Ibid.* In 1971 Congress enacted P.L. 92-224, the Emergency Unemployment Compensation Act of 1971 which provided claimants who exhausted regular and extended benefits up to 13 weeks of federally financed temporary compensation making a possible total of 52 weeks. These benefits, payable from January 1972 through March 1973, were available only in states that triggered "on" under special triggers. In December 1974, Congress enacted the Emergency Unemployment Compensation Act of 1974 (P.L. 93-572). As amended, this program provid-

ed Federal Supplemental Benefits (FSB) up to 13 weeks initially, up to 26 weeks (making a possible total benefit payment of 65 weeks) for the period March 1975 through December 1975. Beginning January 1976 through March 1977 FSB paid up to 13 weeks in states with at least 5 percent but less than 6 percent insured unemployment rates (IUR) and up to 26 weeks when the IUR was at least 6 percent. Program was extended through January 1978, but the maximum FSB was reduced from 26 to 13 weeks beginning May 1977. More recently, Congress established a Federal Supplemental Compensation Program (P.L. 97-248) to provide up to 6, 8, or 10 weeks of additional benefits from September 1982 through March 1983. An additional 2 to 6 weeks were added (depending on state IUR) by legislation adopted December 1982 without extending the March 1983 cut-off date. At this writing, it seems likely the date will be extended by Congress.

68. *Congressional Record,* June 30, 1980, Summary of Finance Committee Recommendation, p. S 8916.

69. U.S. Department of Labor, Bureau of Employment Security, *Manual of State Employment Security Legislation* (Washington, DC, revised September 1950), p. C-22.

70. *Congressional Record* (March 4, 1980), Senator Boren, p. S 2094.

71. *Ibid.,* (Senator Levin), p. S 2109.

72. *Manual of State Employment Security Legislation, op. cit.,* p. C-64.

73. *Congressional Record* (June 30, 1980), Senator Williams, p. S 8940.

74. U.S. Department of Labor, Bureau of Employment Security, *Unemployment Insurance Legislative Policy, Recommendations for State Legislation 1962,* BES No. U-212A, October 1962.

75. Statement of Lawrence E. Weatherford, Acting Deputy Assistant for Employment and Training, U.S. Department of Labor, before the Subcommittee on Public Assistance and Unemployment Compensation, Committee on Ways and Means, U.S. House of Representatives, March 12, 1981.

76. *Ibid.*

77. *Ibid.*

78. *Ibid.*

79. Spencer Rich, "Jobless Aid Fraying as a Safety Net," *Washington Post,* November 6, 1982, pp. 1, 10.

80. P.L. 97-248. See footnote 67.

81. *Congressional Record,* August 17, 1982, "Budget Impact of the Provisions to Lower Unemployment Compensation Tax Thresholds and to Provide Federal Supplemental Benefits," Table 4, p. H 6292.

82. P.L. 97-248.

83. *Congressional Record,* August 17, 1982, "Budget Impact of Each Provision Within the Conference Agreement," Table 3, p. H 6291.

84. *Congressional Record,* March 4, 1980 (Senator Javits), p. S 2099.

85. *Ibid.* (Senator Moynihan), p. S 2098.

86. *Ibid.*

Chapter 4
Administration of Federal Standards:
Direct Federal-State Confrontation

Federal statutory enactments are of no consequence at all unless implemented by state legislation. No change of any kind will affect a single worker, claimant or employer unless and until the state UI law is amended to reflect that change.[1] In converting Congressional mandate to actual practice, federal-state confrontation occurs directly and frequently. How that confrontation arises and is resolved, the parties or machinery involved at the state and federal levels, and trends in experience over the years constitute the subject matter of this chapter.

State Legislation

The volume of proposed unemployment insurance legislation in all states averages about 2,000 bills a year. The number varies widely year to year, particularly in relation to the volume of federal UI amendments and the consequent need for implementing state legislation. In most states, when conforming legislation is needed, the state agency responsible for administering the law takes the initiative for developing a UI legislative program. This unit is the most knowledgeable about the subject matter and usually the only state organization in communication with a federal DOL regional UI office about issues or problems presented by federal requirements. The state administration usually has

127

the bill introduced in the legislature and provides background and support during the legislative proceedings.

This pattern is less likely to be the approach taken in the case of substantive program legislation not involving new federal requirements. In some states, a three or more member advisory council, appointed for staggered terms and representative of labor, management and the public, plays an active (and in some states a dominating) role in the development of UI legislative programs. In such cases, the state agency provides technical advice to the council, particularly on conformity matters. In a few states, legislative committees assume a leadership role in formulating UI legislative programs.

In all states, interest groups attempt to influence the fate of bills that may affect them. Their efforts are reflected in the advisory council and in appropriate legislative committees. As in other areas, their success in UI varies greatly depending on their expertise, popularity, organizational and financial strengths, with the most important determinant usually being the quality of opposing interest groups, if any. Management groups are usually more effective than labor in UI. They have a concrete objective (lowering costs) that sustains an interest in all aspects of UI. State labor organizations seem usually less interested in UI than workers' compensation, and theirs has often been a single issue (e.g., maximum weekly benefit amount) focus. This may be because they usually have less staff and fewer resources for lobbying efforts than their management counterparts. Nor is there the same close consensus among labor representatives on such issues as disqualification penalties as exists among business groups.

In some states, the fate of UI legislation is often greatly influenced by the dominant personalities of a few persons or even a single individual. It may be a state agency representative, an employer, an employers' group representative, or, less frequently, a representative of a labor group. Characteristically, these individuals have long experience, great expertise, and command wide confidence and influence.

There are, of course, many variations of these patterns, even within a single state at different times. There are considerable variations also in the quality of legislative drafting among the states. A number of factors are responsible. Larger states with legislatures regularly in session often have more specialized committees, more skilled staff continuity and, accordingly, more knowledge and experience in both the subject matter and legislative drafting. But even in larger states, regularly occurring changes in the political climate determine the composition of the legislature, its committees and staff, as well as the executive branch and agency officials. Given the program's complexity, frequent change of key legislative and executive personnel makes difficult the accumulation of the knowledge and understanding necessary to produce sound laws.

In any event, a relatively large number of bills are poorly drafted. They may be incomplete or simply too ambiguous to accomplish the framer's intent. One of the most common problems is for the author of an amendment to a state law provision to neglect to take account of its implications for other elements of the law. The various components of benefit formulas, particularly, are interdependent and changes in one aspect may have an automatic and sometimes undesirable impact on other aspects. A simple increase in a state's maximum weekly benefit amount may affect qualifying requirements, benefit duration, partial benefits, and disqualification provisions. With a qualifying requirement, for example, expressed as a multiple of the weekly benefit amount (as in almost one-third of the states), an increase in the maximum will result automatically in an increase in the qualifying wages for the maximum. In most states where the number of weeks benefits are payable is determined by dividing the total amount of entitlement (set as a specified proportion, usually one-third, of total base-period earnings) by the weekly benefit amount, an increase in weekly amounts may translate into fewer weeks or payments for many claimants. An increase in the maximum weekly benefit will have implications in states where partial earnings limits and disqualifications are expressed as multiples of the individual's weekly benefit amount.

Although the secondary impacts are often anticipated, this is not always true; and the results are not always desirable, as when, for example, an increase in the minimum weekly benefit results in substantial numbers of unemployed workers failing to meet the minimum qualifying requirement, or when an increase in the maximum weekly benefit results in individuals with substantial high quarter earnings failing to qualify for any benefits.[2]

Federal Review of Proposed State Legislation

As of 1983, a staff of two or three skilled legislative analysts in the Department of Labor's Unemployment Insurance Service reviews proposed state UI legislation for conformity with federal law. The bills come directly from the state UI agency to the UIS pursuant to the Secretary of Labor's responsibility for certifying each state's law for tax credit or administrative grants. A second source of UI bills is Commerce Clearing House, and a third source is DOL's regional offices. The review is not confined to conformity. The staff comments on the technical adequacy of a bill. At least until 1982, when it seems that the practice was suspended, they also made recommendations with respect to the bill from a policy standpoint. The responsibilities of this unit extend to negotiating the resolution of issues if a problem bill is actually enacted. Finally, if it comes to that, they are responsible for developing support for DOL's position in a hearing on state legislation containing conformity issues. This activity of the UIS is described in some detail because it is a critical factor in maintaining a viable federal-state partnership.

The UIS staff works closely with the one or two attorneys from DOL's Solicitor's Office assigned to unemployment insurance. Earlier in its history, Solicitor's Office staff assigned this responsibility was much larger and played a significant role in the review process. All communications by UIS to the states directly or through the regional offices were required to be "cleared" with the Solicitor's Office before release. The resulting delays and internal disputes were tolerable when issues were relatively few and generally confined to technical experience rating proposals. The procedure was abandoned when the volume of federal UI legislation and subsequent issues increased significantly as a result of the 1970 and 1976 amendments. By 1980, the UIS-Solicitor's Office relationship became more analogous to a conventional lawyer-client arrangement, with clearance generally confined only to maturing conformity issues, and with the UIS selecting the issues on which it seeks advice or interpretation.

DOL regional office staff dealing with UI matters also participate in the legislative review process, but the extent of their involvement varies substantially among regions. It depends on their interest, their skill in this area, the pressure of other business, and their relations with their "client" state agencies. Some regional offices operate only as transmission belts, forwarding bills and whatever relevant information is available to the National Office and transmitting National Office reactions to the state agencies. Others play an active role not only in the review process (adding often valuable observations to other information about bills they send to the National Office) but also in the promotion of needed or desirable legislation, and in "translating" National Office comments to the state agencies, not to change the substance of the communication, but either to personalize the response or to add or soften emphasis where appropriate from their standpoint.

Some regional offices have acquired a paternal, protective relationship with their state agencies. Others share their state agencies' negative attitudes toward National Office communications. Both types tend to defend state actions, diminish the significance of nonconformity issues, and seek compromise favorable to the states in the resolution of conflicts. Most regional offices, however, invariably adopt National Office positions as their own, and some are vigorous and highly skilled proponents of DOL positions on specific state bills. No regional office presumes to act independently of the National Office on state legislation except in the case of familiar, routine bills which have been the subject of previous correspondence. On the other hand, no regional office welcomes direct state agency-National Office communications except in occasional situations where contact needs to be quick and the subject is highly technical or complicated.

The regional offices that are knowledgeable in the legislative area provide a valuable service in helping the National Office assess the prospects of conflict-producing legislation. They are often aware of the motivation of the bill's sponsor, the political climate in the state legislature and the Governor's position on the bill. Not the least of their contributions is information they provide about the intent of bills that may be so ambiguous or obscure as to defy analysis. Some state agencies provide a thorough analysis of unemployment insurance bills for the benefit of their administrations or advisory councils and these are usually forwarded to the National Office.

Review Priorities

The small percentage of the thousands of UI amendments introduced each year that actually are reviewed carefully by the UIS legislative analysts are the bills that state agencies or regional offices indicate will receive serious consideration by the states' legislatures. These include state administration-backed bills (particularly those designed to implement federal law requirements), bills introduced by influential legislators or on behalf of established interest groups, and bills supported by the state's advisory council on unemployment insurance. Bills not identified as likely to receive serious consideration are not usually analyzed unless they contain obvious or serious conformity issues or unless they begin to receive favorable action. State agencies' indications of probable legislative activity are only preliminary estimates. The analysts' priorities may change as bills begin to move through the legislative process. Each action taken on a bill, as well as copies of each introduced bill and its amendments are communicated on a reasonably current basis to the UIS by Commerce Clearing House (CCH), a private organization headquartered in Chicago. This is a service subscribed to by the UIS and funded from the DOL budget.

Since bills may sometimes move quickly through a legislature, the CCH "action sheets" showing the status of a bill will reveal what new bills will need review and also dictate the analysts' priorities and the means they use for communicating comments on issues. A matter involving technical corrections of a bill will be shelved temporarily to treat a bill with provisions that are undesirable from a policy standpoint. These bills will in turn be sidetracked in order to give priority to a bill that has strong support, particularly if comments were specifically requested by the state agency. This priority will yield to a bill containing a conformity issue, and all other actions will be suspended, if necessary, to handle a potential conformity issue in a bill that has been reported favorably by a committee or already passed one House of the state legislature. As each of the more demanding priorities is satisfied, attention reverts to the less urgent matters.

Technical Adequacy

The review of state legislation is not easy. Unemployment insurance is a very complicated program, with 53 variations of each major ingredient. Nearly fifty years of precedent decisions, recent comprehensive changes in federal laws, innumerable interpretations and policy positions take time to absorb. Another skill, that of applying federal requirements to proposed state legislation, takes long experience. The ability to communicate opinions, either orally or in writing, clearly and succinctly takes time to develop. It is usually a minimum of two years before a UIS analyst can handle even routine reviews and correspondence without close supervision.

Many state legislative proposals are technically inadequate. Ambiguous language, misplaced punctuation, missing sentences, inappropriate positioning, erroneous citations, are not uncommon. These are in addition to the most common failing, already mentioned, of neglecting to take account of the implications of a proposed amendment on other, interrelated elements of the program.

Legislative drafting skills are certainly not confined to federal officials, but DOL technicians have an advantage over most of their state counterparts simply because they are continuously engaged in reviewing and commenting on proposed and enacted UI legislation from 53 jurisdictions. The advantage is most obvious when enactment of new state legislation is necessary to implement federal law requirements. Following adoption of any changes in federal law requirements or definitions, DOL develops suggested draft language for states that will conform with the new amendments. Federal technicians will thus have already considered the disadvantages of deviations from the recommended language. Moreover, they are more likely to have a better understanding of precisely what is required, since the new federal requirements may well have been drafted by them originally, and in any event, they will usually have had more direct knowledge than state officials of the relevant legislative history. Accordingly, it is common for states to adopt suggested DOL draft language either verbatim or with no more changes than the minor adjustments necessary to tailor the language to the peculiarities of each state law.

In matters solely within the scope of state jurisdiction, federal recommendations on program policy may go unheeded, but DOL advice on technical adequacy is usually welcome and followed. If a proposed state amendment will conflict with federal requirements, federal technicians may offer alternative language that will serve the intent of the sponsor, consistent with federal law, even if DOL considers the result undesirable from a program standpoint.

Program Policy

The same degree of state acceptance of DOL technical suggestions does not extend to recommendations for program improvements. In many, if not most, states, qualifying requirements, eligibility conditions, disqualifications, benefit duration, and benefit formulas are more often the result of labor-management negotiations and compromises than careful evaluation of the merits. A common compromise, for example, involves trading an increase in the maximum weekly benefit amount in return for a tightening of the eligibility or disqualification requirements. Benefit increases are often simply not possible without concomitant actions to minimize costs.

Undeterred by the usually cool reception it receives to its program recommendations, DOL has in the past continued to urge states to adopt its recommendations for a sound program. They range from key program elements (e.g., maximum weekly benefit should equal two-thirds of the statewide average weekly wage) to highly technical matters (e.g., for qualifying requirements, the specified minimum required high-quarter wage should not exceed one-fourth of the minimum base-period wage required, so that no claimant who meets the latter requirement will be denied benefits solely because his base-period earnings were distributed evenly among the four quarters of the base period).[3]

The latest comprehensive compilation of DOL policy recommendations, issued in 1962,[4] still constitutes DOL policy on benefit formulas and other matters not subsequently affected by federal legislation. Until the late 1970s, DOL vigorously advanced policy recommendations, in reacting to specific individual state legislative proposals, and through general legislative planning sessions. Following the 1970 and 1976 federal amendments, for example, DOL exploited the opportunity to capitalize on states' interest in the new legislation by conducting nationwide seminars for state agency officials and not only explaining new conformity conditions but also advocating improvements in program areas untouched by Congress. Some state agencies that agreed with DOL were successful in getting improvements enacted, perhaps because of the heavy volume of necessary legislation and the confusion that regularly exists between amendments required for conformity and those advanced only on a policy basis.

Since the 1976 seminars, there has been a hiatus in DOL's active advocacy of program policy recommendations. The 1974-76 recession and the consequent depletion of funds in several states produced an inhospitable climate for DOL's benefit duration and disqualification recommendations.

Many otherwise sympathetic state agencies were apprehensive that any attempt to amend the state UI law would serve only to provide an opportunity for the introduction of restrictive legislation. In addition, DOL was somewhat committed to delaying any major recommendations, pending the Final Report of the National Commission on Unemployment Compensation (NCUC).

Diminished DOL policy pushing was also due to the 1970 and 1976 federal amendments. Creation in 1970 of the permanent program of extended benefits left states little incentive to extend regular duration beyond 26 weeks, or even to liberalize their duration formulas. Extensions of coverage mandated by the federal amendments left relatively few jobs still unprotected, thereby reducing the need to press the states to expand coverage on their own. The three remaining major program policy areas, benefit adequacy, fund solvency, and disqualification severity, not yet preempted by federal amendments, offered little promise. Most states had already adopted the recommended "escalator" concept of tying the maximum weekly benefit amount directly to changes in the statewide average weekly wage so that a change in the latter automatically produces a change in the former. By 1978, about a dozen states had established the maximum as an amount equal to as much as two-thirds of the statewide wage, the recommended level. But any further improvements in benefit amount and duration seemed unlikely, at least until many states' programs were on a firmer financial footing.

States have also been reluctant to adopt DOL recommendations on tax and financing provisions. This advice generally concentrated on the need for each state to establish an adequate reserve, and offered as a guideline a measure based on the state's past experience. Such a reserve, it was suggested, taken as a percent of total payrolls in the state, should equal at least one and one-half times the highest benefit cost rate (total benefit outlays as a percent of payrolls) in any 12-month period during the preceding ten or more years. While proportionately more states adhering to the guideline avoided the need to borrow than those with reserve levels below this minimum, not all states that followed the guidelines succeeded in remaining solvent.

Federal financing recommendations also stressed methods for predetermining annual tax yields, having higher or lower tax rate schedules take effect in response to realistic fund level measures (e.g., reserves as ratios of total payrolls rather than as fixed dollar amounts made obsolete by inflation), ensuring adequate financing of pooled costs (noncharged benefits and benefits ineffectively charged to employers already at the maximum rate) through a reasonable minimum or surtax rate.

In recent years, financing recommendations have been aimed largely at assisting debtor states to evaluate the options available in repaying loans, regaining solvency as quickly as possible, and maintaining adequate reserves on a long term basis. Of course, the expansion of federal loan repayment requirements has moved the federal-state dialogue in regard to financing beyond the advisory level.

Even in good times, DOL was never successful in persuading states to adopt its recommendations on disqualifications. DOL had always urged that a disqualification for voluntary quit, discharge for misconduct, or refusal of suitable work should result in denial of benefits only for the period of unemployment presumed attributed to the claimant's own action, or about six weeks, the length of the average spell of unemployment. After that period, the individual's continued unemployment could reasonably be considered due to economic conditions and, therefore, compensable. Most states consistently rejected this concept, preferring instead to consider a disqualification as punishment for irresponsible action.

The cessation of DOL policy recommendations was also attributable to personnel changes within the Labor Department. UIS staff had been steadily reduced over the years. The number of analysts responsible for reviewing and commenting on state legislation was cut from eight to four. The number of attorneys in the Solicitor's Office solely responsible for unemployment insurance matters was reduced from six to one. Corresponding reductions were made in the research staff. UIS library facilities were eliminated entirely. Perhaps most significant, virtually every UIS staff member with long experience in the program, some dating back to its origin (and usually with a correspondingly firm commitment to its original principles and orientation), was gone by 1980. Beginning that year, the UIS was headed for the first time by an individual with no prior UI background, operating under a hierarchy of officials for whom the unemployment insurance program was clearly not a high priority. During this period, the UIS and even DOL became considerably less influential than the Office of Management and Budget, for example, in determining unemployment insurance policy.

Finally, by 1982, the making of policy recommendations by staff on state legislation seems to have been discontinued. This includes even recommendations which simply follow established policy as contained in the draft bills or the comprehensive DOL policy statement issued in 1962.

Conformity

Only once has a state been assessed any penalty for nonconformity with FUTA provisions. Only twice have administrative grants been withheld for violations of Social Security Act provisions, and then only for brief periods. It is rare for an issue even to go to a hearing, as evidenced by a history of only about a dozen conformity hearings since 1937.

The infrequency of hearings is certainly not due to the lack of serious issues. Each year there may be as many as 50 potential conformity issues presented by proposed or enacted state legislation and a residue of 15 to 20 actual issues requiring negotiation. The small number of hearings is due primarily to the mutual interest of both levels of government to avoid formal confrontations that could produce disadvantages for both. For the state, an adverse Secretary's decision means either sanctions or, if they are to be avoided, capitulation and a change in law or practive which the state does not really want. At stake for DOL is the potential, exercised on a few past occasions, of Congressional intervention, possibly with a consequent diminution of the Secretary's authority.[5]

To keep the number of serious confrontations to a minimum, it is not enough for the two levels of government simply to share an interest in this objective. Other factors must also be present, including a federal staff skilled in detecting issues, communicating opinions and reasons, and initiating and negotiating solutions. Nor is it always enough that issues are settled. Resolution of an issue—on the grounds of political expediency, or intimidation, or on any other basis than the best available judgment of what the federal law requires and the most practical means of achieving conformity—is only a temporary settlement.

Identifying Issues

It is very unusual for an issue to be overlooked, although the likelihood increases as federal review staff and resources are reduced. A major incentive to be thorough is the known difficulty and embarrassment involved in trying to persuade a state legislature to remove a conflicting provision from its law when no indication had been made of the existence of an issue at the time the bill was still pending and there was opportunity to defeat or amend it. Because of its staff's familiarity with the federal law, it is also very unusual for DOL to be successfully challenged on an allegation of non-conformity. Conformity issues are not raised lightly by analysts; issues are always raised with the recognition that it may be necessary to defend their position at a hearing. If the analysts are not confident of their position, they will advise the state that the possibility of a conformity issue is being explored and hope that because of the doubt raised, the bill will not survive.

A typical memorandum will pinpoint the language of the bill that raises an issue, describes DOL's understanding of the language and its intent; cite applicable federal law provisions and their interpretations; and describe as clearly as possible the basis for the opinion that if the provision is enacted, the state law, as so amended, will not meet federal law requirements. The DOL analysis is always expressed as an opinion, since only the Secretary can decide that a provision is out of conformity, and then only after he has notified the Governor, extended to the agency an opportunity for hearing, conducted a hearing, if one is desired, and submitted his findings to the state. If there does not appear to be time for a written communication, the UIS may wire its opinion directly to the state agency, or it may telephone state agency officials either directly or in concert with the regional office. If a bill with a serious issue is enacted, the UIS may request the Governor to veto it. All communications will contain full explanations of the reason for DOL's opinion.

Reactions by state agency officials to DOL comments concerning the conformity of pending state legislation range from relief to hostility. Experienced state officials are seldom surprised by a DOL position. In many cases they will have been alerted to the possibility of an issue being raised by the regional office on an informal basis, usually after a quick consultation with National Office staff. Often, the state agency officials will request an opinion on the conformity of a questionable bill. State officials have a considerable incentive in making sure the state legislature knows at an early stage about any potential conformity issues associated with a bill. It is very awkward for state officials who have not given their legislature the DOL warning at the earliest opportunity to advise against enactment of a problem bill that has already gained momentum.

Most bills containing conformity issues are not administration bills or even supported by the state administration. Often they would create serious administrative problems for the agency if they were enacted, or otherwise disrupt established practices or principles. It is not uncommon for state agency officials informally to express the hope that federal analysts will somehow find a conformity issue in the bill so that DOL, rather than state agency officials, will bear responsibility for its defeat. For example, from time to time several states have sought to combine in one organizational structure all state administrative adjudicatory functions and staff, including unemployment insurance referees as well as hearings officers in workers' compensation and other state programs. DOL has recommended strongly against this approach as inimical to both the quality and the promptness of UI hearings. But to the disappointment of state agency officials, DOL has found no basis for challenging the conformity of such a practice, provided federal performance standards are met and granted funds are used only to meet UI responsibilities.

A hostile reaction to a negative DOL opinion on the conformity of a provision sometimes occurs but is unusual even among state agency officials who disagree with the federal position. When such a reaction has occurred, it has often been a manifestation of an underlying animosity toward all federal intervention in state affairs. Generally, an indication from DOL that enactment of a pending bill would present a question of conformity with federal law is recognized as reflecting the DOL analysts' best judgment. It is accepted if the reason for the opinion seems persuasive, and it is usually enough to deter enactment of the vast majority of problem bills.

Avoiding Confrontation

If it appears that a bill posing a conformity issue will be enacted despite DOL recommendations that it be defeated, withdrawn or amended, the state is usually urged to adopt a "savings clause" along with the bill. The one recommended by DOL provides that the provision in question will not take effect unless and until the Secretary of Labor finds that it is consistent with federal law requirements. Adoption of this type of savings clause gives the Secretary ample time to act and avoids the necessity of a conformity hearing. Although DOL is often successful in persuading a state to adopt a savings clause, usually the clause provides that the challenged provision will become effective unless and until the Secretary finds the provision inconsistent with federal law requirements—rather than DOL's version.

The advantage of any savings clause is that it permits a provision to become null and void without further action by the legislature. This can be important to a state confronted with an adverse decision by the Secretary issued during a period when the state legislature is not in session. It is also advantageous to DOL since it obviates the possibility of a sanction, and it usually ends the issue without judicial review. A number of states have rejected adoption of any kind of a savings clause on the grounds that by allowing the fate of an amendment to be determined by the Secretary of Labor, it constitutes an unconstitutional delegation of legislative authority.

Once a bill containing a conformity issue is enacted. DOL will usually request an opinion from the state agency or the state's attorney general as to how it will be interpreted; DOL will advise the state if there is a possible interpretation of the law or the provision that will avoid the issue. For example, as indicated in the preceding chapter, some states amended their definition of suitable work to include *any* job paying the higher of the minimum wage or the claimant's weekly benefit. However, both federal and state laws prohibit disqualification of a claimant for refusing a job paying less than the prevailing wage for such jobs. To avoid an issue that could be raised if an individual were disqualified for turning down a job that paid the minimum wage but not the prevailing wage, DOL recommended that the states interpret their laws as requiring disqualification for refusal of a minimum wage job only if that wage was also the prevailing wage for that type of work.

A more common attempt to avoid a conformity issue by interpretation concerns the so-called automatic coverage provisions in most state laws which require that any employment that is either subject to the FUTA or required by the FUTA to be covered under state law as a condition for tax credit shall be considered covered under state law. Upon enactment by the state of a bill excluding services that are required by federal law to be covered, DOL will ask if the state law will be interpreted to make the automatic coverage requirement controlling.

Less dependable a basis for avoiding a conformity issue are general savings clauses in some state laws that provide for the automatic nullification of any provision found by the Secretary to be inconsistent with federal requirements for tax credit or administrative grants. On the few occasions when it would have been helpful, DOL has not succeeded in persuading states to apply this provision. On the other hand, there have been occasions when a flexible attorney general has found an interpretation never contemplated by DOL. In one instance, a problem provision was interpreted to have a meaning opposite from that suggested by its crystal clear language, on the grounds that the state legislature would never knowingly have enacted a bill that would jeopardize employers' tax credits.

Infrequently, DOL will recede from a position by changing its interpretation of the federal law. For example, a position held for many years that federal law bars states from relieving employers of benefit charges to their accounts (which could affect their tax rates) for unemployment caused by so-called "Acts of God." DOL had argued that natural calamities such as earthquakes and storms were part of the risk of doing business. The fact that such unemployment was beyond an employer's control was not persuasive, since most unemployment is regarded as beyond an employer's control. In 1972 a severe flood caused considerable disruption and job dislocations in Pennsylvania and other states. DOL was persuaded to adjust its position at least to the extent of permitting noncharging of benefits paid for unemployment if caused by a natural disaster declared as such by the President pursuant to the terms of the Disaster Relief Act.

Even more infrequently, DOL will agree not to pursue an issue of nonconformity. This occurs usually only when the offending provision has limited, temporary application. For example, in 1973, New York law was amended to permit noncharging to reimbursing employers of benefits paid over a one-year period to former employees unemployed because of a flood. Up to that time DOL interpreted federal law as prohibiting any noncharging of employers financing benefits on a reimbursable basis. However, since the noncharging in the New York case was a one-time situation, and since the Department itself then intended to seek a change in federal law permitting the practice, the issue was not pursued. Occasionally, a state court will decide a case on the basis of an interpretation of the state UI law that will present a conformity issue. DOL will sometimes not pursue the issue if the state agency can convince the Department that the court's decision has no applicability other than to the instant case, that the state will continue to adhere to a conforming interpretation and that it will appeal the court's ruling, if possible.

Resolution of Issues

With these few exceptions, conformity issues that are once raised with a state are pursued until they are resolved. There is no single approach to resolution. One determining factor will be the seriousness of the issue, as indicated by factors such as the number of individuals affected, the impact on claimants or employers, and the potential consequences to the program. For example, the South Dakota issue described below satisfied all criteria. So did the failure of some states to extend coverage to church-supported schools, as required by the 1976 federal law amendments, according to DOL interpretation. These are usually the most difficult to settle. The South Dakota issue, for example, took two and one-half years to resolve. Even more time can be expected if a state seeks judicial review of a Secretary's adverse determination, as in the case of the church schools issue. In light of these delays, if DOL fails to achieve at least a temporary suspension of a serious nonconforming provision, it will quickly begin the procedures that culminate in a hearing.

The pattern followed is different in the case of less serious matters which constitute the large majority of issues. Instead of moving directly toward a formal confrontation, DOL will follow a variety of alternate roads to eventual settlement which will avoid the burden and risks involved in a hearing. The most common approach is to determine if the state agency and presumably the state administration will introduce and support a bill next year that will correct the problem. If the agency agrees, and concurrence is reached on the language of the corrective legislation, DOL will hold the issue in abeyance until next year's state legislature has had an opportunity to act on the bill. Failure of the legislature to correct the issue will usually set in motion the procedures for a hearing.

The law requires that the Secretary of Labor certify to the Secretary of the Treasury on October 31 of each year all states whose laws have been approved so that employers may receive credit against the federal tax. The Secretary of Labor cannot deny certifying a state law for tax offset credit and cannot withhold administrative funds until the state agency has had an opportunity for hearing. There are built-in time constraints in the federal laws for each step between notification to the Governor of the issue, notice of hearing, scheduling the hearing, exchange of briefs, mailing of proposed decisions, issuance of the administrative law judge's recommended decision, Secretary's decision, and opportunity for judicial review. The result is that unless the initial steps are taken by early summer, the state's law must be certified on October 31 and the issue moves over to the following year. Usually, the state legislature will then have another opportunity to correct the problem. If it does so within a reasonable time, the issue will be resolved. Although the October 31 deadline does not apply to issues involving the possible denial of granted administrative funds, there are still substantial delays between notification of an issue and the application of that sanction.

The issues that linger the longest are often relatively minor problems that could be corrected by a change in state agency regulations or procedures. If the state agency is not really interested in making the necessary change, and DOL is reluctant to go to a hearing because the issue is not important enough to warrant the time and work, the conforming changes can be delayed almost indefinitely. Resolution of such an issue may well await the eventual appointment of new, more amenable state agency leadership. One of the longest continuing issues involves a state's regulations which apply different filing and reporting requirements to partially unemployed claimants (claimants entitled to a reduced or partial unemployment benefit for a week in which some wages were earned but less than a specified amount) than those prescribed in the federal *Employment Security Manual.* This document contains interpretations of federal law requirements and spells out acceptable state practice in various administrative situations. Before a nonconformity hearing on the state's regulations can even be scheduled, the *Manual* prescribes a procedure requiring federal evaluation of whether the state provisions, while differing from the suggested *Manual* provisions, could nevertheless still be considered consistent with federal law. The evaluation must be made in concert with state authorities. This particular issue has remained unresolved for almost a decade, although there have been several exchanges of proposed regulations and comments over the years.

A number of personal factors also influence success in resolving issues short of a hearing. Mutual respect between federal staff (regional and national) and state agency officials as well as competence in the art of negotiation can be critical. Conversely, heavy pressure ordinarily has negative results. The application of pressure on a Secretary by the state's legislative delegation, for example, usually has no effect. But this is not invariable. There have been instances where a change in federal position appears to have been influenced by political pressure.

The traditional pattern of resolving most issues prior to a hearing may be altered in the future. First, the federal standards enacted in 1980 as well as additional amendments enacted in 1981 are viewed by many states as serious and threatening intrusions into state authority. Unlike the comprehensive amendments enacted in 1970 and 1976, there was neither opportunity nor effort made in 1980 to obtain and consider reactions from the states either individually or through the Interstate Conference of Employment Security Agencies (ICESA). Moreover, some states considered unreasonable the short deadlines imposed for implementation of the amendments (matter of a few months in some cases), in contrast to the two-year period that is usually permitted. Second, since 1970 states have had the opportunity for judicial review of an adverse determination by the Secretary. Only a few states have exercised that right, but in the one instance to date in which the courts ruled against the state in 1980, the consequences were far less severe than the potential penalty.[6] Armed with this precedent, states can now consider contesting a decision with less fear that the full sanctions will be imposed. Finally, the UIS has lost substantial credibility in recent years. its advice is increasingly disregarded. This is due in part to the loss of effective, experienced and authoritative personnel and the consequent deterioration of performance; the relinquishment of leadership to agencies other than DOL, and the consequent reversal of many long-standing policies; and the increasingly frequent pattern of failing to follow up warnings of sanctions or even to pursue issues at all. In any event, the increased frequency of hearings suggests that apprehensions concerning the prospect of a conformity hearing are disappearing.

Many of the elements involved in a conformity case can be illustrated best by examining one in detail. The issue described in the appendix to this chapter is one of the most significant to confront the system. It arose over a proposal for amendment to the South Dakota law which the state agency submitted on June 22, 1962, to the DOL regional office in Kansas City for comment. The issue was resolved December 11, 1964.

The chronology of the South Dakota issue documents some of the common approaches toward resolution of an issue prior to a hearing, including informal attempts of each party to persuade the other, consideration of alternative provisions, and adoption of a savings clause that appeared to invite a determinative DOL decision on the basis of an informal hearing.[7]

The chronology also shows the development of strategy by each party, including the utilization of interest groups, congressmen and other state agencies. None of these efforts was successful in heading off a hearing. Why did resolution of this issue (and only about a dozen others) require a hearing, while many hundreds of other issues have been resolved informally, including almost identical issues in other states at other times? Certainly the following factors contributed: the Governor's support of the questioned amendment; potentially significant savings in benefit costs, and consequent strong support by business groups; strong convictions concerning federal versus state authority by proponents and opponents of the amendment; and the existence of more than one contentious issue.

Whatever disadvantage the state incurred because the hearing was conducted in Washington, by a federal administrative law judge, on the basis of which the decision as to the state's conformity with federal law is made by the U.S. Secretary of Labor, was eliminated six years after the South Dakota hearing by amendment of the federal law (Public Law 91-373) under which a state may seek judicial review of an adverse Secretary's decision.

Appendix to Chapter 4
Chronology and Anatomy of a Conformity Case

6-22-62 P.J. Maloney, Commissioner and Counsel of the South Dakota Employment Security Department, submitted a legislative proposal to the Kansas City Regional Administrator of DOL's Bureau of Employment Security, for comment. The proposed amendment would effectively deny payment of unemployment insurance to claimants by lengthening the waiting period from 1 week to 7 to 13 weeks, depending on the amount of the claimant's base-period earnings. Only those who earned $6,000 or more would be subject to the proposed benefit postponement schedule:

Amount of base-period earnings	Number of weeks of benefit delay
$6,000 - 6,999.99	7
7,000 - 7,999.99	9
8,000 - 8,999.99	11
9,000 - over	13

6-29-62 The Regional Administrator's response advised Maloney that the proposed amendment would raise questions of conformity. The amendment injects a consideration of "need" as a condition of eligibility for benefits. Under the proposal, benefits would not be paid solely with respect to unemployment, as required by federal law.

The regional office mailed a memorandum to Robert C. Goodwin, Administrator, Bureau of Employment Security, attaching copies of the agency's letter and the Regional Administrator's response.

7-20-62 Memorandum from William Norwood, National UI Office, Director, UIS, to the Regional Director advised that the National Office concurs with the June 29, 1962 regional office letter to the state and provided further comment in

support of the position along the following lines: The prohibition against a needs test as a condition for the payment
of compensation is implicit in the FUTA definition of "compensation." Sections 303(a)(5) of the Social Security Act and
3304(a)(4) of the FUTA require, as a condition for the certification of state unemployment insurance laws, that such
laws provide for the use of all moneys withdrawn from the
state unemployment funds solely in the payment of
unemployment compensation, with certain exceptions not
relevant to the present problem. "Compensation" as defined
in Section 3306(h), FUTA, means "cash benefits payable to
individuals with respect to their unemployment." This
limitation on the expenditure of moneys withdrawn from
unemployment compensation funds negates, by necessary
implication, the disbursement of such moneys on a needs
basis.

7-25-62 Letter from Regional Administrator to Maloney
transmitted the National Office comments and reasserted
that the proposed legislation would raise a question of conformity.

7-31-62 Agency response from J.V. Yaukey, South Dakota
Chief of Benefits, to Regional Administrator advised that
the proposed amendment had the support of several large
and influential employers in the state who are trying to solve
the problem of paying benefits in the winter months every
year to claimants who consistently earn high wages plus
overtime about nine months of the year and then draw
unemployment benefits for the remaining three months,
even though they had already put in a full year's quota of
hours worked. The agency requested a counter-suggestion as
to how to solve this problem.

8-3-62 Charles Wilkins, UIS Regional Director in Kansas City, transmitted agency letter to UIS, National Office (Norwood) with a request for assistance.

8-24-62 Norwood's response reiterated the position that the proposal to increase the waiting period for claimants whose base-period earnings exceed $6,000 would introduce the concept of "need" as a condition of eligibility and would present a question of conformity with federal law. The memorandum advised that although the Bureau was reluctant to recommend seasonality provisions because of the difficulty of administering them equitably and effectively, it was submitting a draft seasonality provision for the agency's consideration that would provide a better solution to the state's problem than the proposed amendment.

9-4-62 Letter from Wilkins transmitted to Maloney the National Office comments and the suggested seasonality provision.

9-10-62 Letter, Yaukey to Regional Administrator, argued that the Bureau is looking at the "needs" test concept too narrowly. It rejected the seasonality provision because it would be "devastating in its effect on low income people" while the additional waiting period proposal "would probably not affect more than 100 or 150 claimants."

9-18-62 Wilkins' letter to Maloney advised that the National Office was preparing comments and attached a copy of an earlier Bureau paper entitled "Entitlement to Unemployment Benefits Based on Consideration Involving Need: Conformity with Requirements of Federal Law." This monograph was prepared by DOL National Office staff and distributed at a legislative meeting held in Kansas City in 1961.

9-19-62 Wilkins transmitted to Norwood copies of the latest correspondence as well as a report of a discussion with state agency officials indicating the agency's belief that dependents' allowances added by some states to weekly benefits are based as much on need as the proposed amendment, and yet they are not held out of conformity.

10-8-62 National Office (Norwood) memorandum to the regional office (Wilkins) referred to the article, "The Means Test and Dependents' Allowances" in the July 1961 issue of the *Employment Security Review,* a monthly publication of the Department of Labor, reiterated the Bureau's position and explained again why it believes the proposal in question does not meet the requirements of federal law. The memorandum pointed out that the position taken is consistent with prior advice given other states and disagreed that the suggested seasonality provision would unjustly deny benefits to low-income workers.

10-24-62 Letter to state agency from regional office discussed desirable legislation for the 1963 legislative session and recommended against adoption of the increased waiting week proposal.

11-16-62 Memorandum to Norwood from Wilkins transmitted a savings clause that the agency wished to add to the proposed amendment. It provided that the provision would be inoperative if on or before January 2, 1964, the Secretary of Labor found it inconsistent with federal law.

12-10-62 Wilkins informed Norwood that the State Advisory Council approved the proposal on November 28, 1962. He also forwarded a copy of an agency study indicating that in a nine-month period, about 4 percent of claimants would be affected and in a 12-month period, there would be a reduction of $45,000 in benefits paid. The regional office also transmitted copies of a letter to the agency from an attorney for the Greater South Dakota Association, an organization of businessmen, supporting the proposal. Wilkins advised that the proposal probably would be enacted during the 1963 legislative session.

12-21-62 National Office telephone call to Wilkins advised that suggested language for a savings clause would be mailed within a few days. This followed a December 17, 1963 memorandum to the Bureau from the Solicitor's Office suggesting revisions in the Bureau's proposed language.

12-16-62 Memorandum from Bureau Director (Goodwin) advised Norwood (Director, UIS) of a call from Assistant Director of the Social Security Department of the AFL-CIO, Ray Munts, concerning the state proposal and requesting information about the issue.

12-27-62 National Office (UIS) memorandum to regional office suggested a savings clause under which the operation of the amendment would be made conditional upon the Secretary's finding that the amendment was consistent with federal requirements. The memorandum advised that if the agency continued to support the savings clause it had proposed, at least reference to a specific date in the clause should be omitted.

1-1-63 Wilkins advised the National Office by phone that the agency had rejected the DOL-suggested savings clause and supported a clause providing that the proposal would become effective January 1, 1964, unless, prior to January 2, 1964, the Secretary found that the proposal failed to meet federal law requirements.

1-4-63 Wilkins transmitted to Norwood the South Dakota legislative proposal together with other bills that had been introduced.

1-28-63 Memorandum from Bureau Director Goodwin to Secretary of Labor Willard Wirtz informed him "of the background and present status of an issue which may eventually present a question for your determination concerning the conformity of the South Dakota Employment Security Law, as it is expected to be amended, with requirements of the Internal Revenue Code and the Social Security Act."

2-5-63 National Office memorandum informed Wilkins that Commerce Clearing House (CCH) reported that the proposal had been introduced as Senate Bill 89, and that the CCH version of the bill contained erroneous citations to the federal provisions.

3-7-63 Wilkins informed Norwood that Senate Bill 89 had passed both Houses of the state legislature and that Governor Archie Gubbrud was expected to approve it.

3-25-63 Regional office forwarded certification, made March 14, 1963, by the South Dakota Secretary of State, that the attached document was a true, correct and examined copy of Senate Bill 89, as approved by the Governor, March 13, 1963. The bill as enacted included a savings clause which provided that the amendment would become effective on January 15, 1964, unless the United States Secretary of Labor, prior to January 8, 1964, found that it failed to meet the requirements of federal law.

4-29-63 Submittal prepared for Secretary of Labor, with the Solicitor's Office participation, included summations of both state and Bureau arguments, a chronology of development, and a proposed letter to the Governor.

6-13-63 Letter from Goodwin to Maloney advised that the Bureau's recommendations were being prepared for the Secretary's consideration and that a copy of the statement would be furnished the agency July 1, 1963. The letter requested the agency to furnish a statement of its position by July 22 so that an informal hearing could be scheduled during the week of July 29.

6-26-63 Yaukey letter to Wilkins described the Governor's recent speech at a state meeting of the American Legion in which he used as his principal theme federal encroachment on states' rights. Almost 10 minutes of the 25-minute talk was devoted to the conflict over Senate Bill 89. The letter attached an article from a Huron, South Dakota newspaper describing the provision and the issue.

7-1-63 Letter from Goodwin to South Dakota Governor Gubbrud advised that an informal hearing would be scheduled during the week of July 29. The letter enclosed a copy of the Bureau recommendation to the Secretary, "for your information."

7-12-63 Letter from Governor Gubbrud to Secretary Wirtz transmitted a brief on the state's position and requested advice on the date of the hearing.

7-26-63 Letter to Secretary of Labor Wirtz from Cliff W. Shrader, President, South Dakota State Federation of Labor, submitted a brief urging a finding of nonconformity.

7-29-63 Letter to Secretary from U.S. Senator George McGovern of South Dakota indicated receipt of State Federation of Labor brief, urged that it be given full consideration, and requested to be informed of the determination.

8-1-63 "Informal" hearing in Washington between DOL's Administrative Assistant Secretary, Leo R. Werts, as the Secretary's representative and South Dakota agency officials.

8-7-63 Goodwin letter to President Shrader, South Dakota State Federation of Labor, acknowledged receipt of brief.

8-9-63 Letter from Secretary to Senator McGovern indicated that all expressions of opinion would be taken into consideration, including the State Federation of Labor's brief.

8-13-63 Letter from Goodwin to Ben H. Radcliffe, President, South Dakota Farmers Union, responded to 7-31-63 inquiry and advised that Secretary would consider views from all interested parties.

9-3-63 Letter to Secretary Wirtz from Nelson H. Cruikshank, Director, Department of Social Security, AFL-

CIO, transmitted the AFL-CIO's detailed views on the issue, urging a finding of noncomformity.

9-11-63 Secretary's letter to U.S. Senator Karl R. Mundt of South Dakota responded to the Senator's letter of August 29, 1963, which questioned the propriety of DOL's consideration of the state law's conformity with federal law requirements. The Secretary's response described the savings clause which prompted the state agency to request a finding from the Secretary.

9-11-63 Letter, Jeremiah D. Murphy to Leo Werts, submitted a brief on behalf of the Greater South Dakota Association in support of the position taken by the state. Letter contained the assumption that formal hearings on the conformity issue would be held if Werts found that the provision was inconsistent with federal law.

9-25-63 Maloney to Werts transmitted final summary of the state's arguments.

10-8-63 Letter, Werts to Murphy, advised that the certification of the state law for tax credit and administrative grants was not at issue since Senate Bill 89 provided that if the Secretary found that the provision did not meet federal law requirements, the provision would become inoperative and not part of the state law. Since state law certification was not at issue, there was no provision in federal law for a hearing, although the state had already been given a full opportunity to present its views. Accordingly, no further hearing would be held.

1-3-64 Letter from Secretary Wirtz to Governor Gubbrud advised that "After careful consideration, I have concluded that Senate Bill 89 is not consistent with the requirements of the Social Security Act and the Federal Unemployment Tax Act." The basis for the conclusion included legislative history showing that Congress intended unemployment, not need or lack of need, to be the test of a worker's eligibility for benefits; that although details such as the length of waiting periods were to be left to the states, they must be consistent with "the fundamental concepts of unemployment insurance and in the context of the cooperative Federal-State system." It argued that the state provision constituted a needs test and that other states' provisions for weighted benefit schedules and dependents' allowances were distinguishable from the South Dakota bill.

1-6-64 A summary of the Secretary's decision was mailed to all UIS Regional Directors.

1-17-64 Memorandum from Ralph Altman, Director, UIS Office of Program Policies and Legislation, to Norwood reported on telephone conversations with Wilkins on developments in South Dakota. Wilkins advised Altman that the State Attorney General was considering a memorandum opinion that Senate Bill 89 was not inoperative because the Secretary had not provided a hearing to South Dakota. Wilkins had advised Yaukey that the state law had already been certified for 1963 tax credits but that the next administrative grant could be affected. The Secretary could either proceed to the grants question alone (which then required no hearing) or proceed to the FUTA question which did require a hearing.

1-20-64 Memorandum, Wilkins to Miller, Deputy Director of the Unemployment Insurance Service, summarized developments in the state following issuance of Secretary's 1-3-64 decision and identified parties interested in pursuing the issue and those ready to accept the Secretary's decision.

1-17-64 Senator Mundt advised Secretary Wirtz of being informed by Mr. Goodwin that the 8-1-63 meeting between Leo Werts and the South Dakota agency officials was not a hearing of record, but rather a preliminary hearing, and that no finding by the Secretary would be forthcoming before a

hearing of record. He questioned why a finding of nonconformity had been issued without adherence to the statutory
provision calling for a formal hearing and why a promise
from Mr. Goodwin, that there would be a hearing of record
before any final action was taken, had been violated.

1-22-64 Letter from Senator Mundt to the Secretary
acknowledged receipt of Secretary's January 17 notification
to him of the nonconformity of the South Dakota provision
with federal law. He reiterated his understanding, from talk-
ing with Mr. Goodwin, that the August 1 meeting was only
informal.

1-28-64 Memorandum to the Secretary from Charles
Donahue, Solicitor of Labor, concluded (1) that the South
Dakota "savings clause" is not an unconstitutional delegation of legislative power to the Secretary, and (2) that South
Dakota could not complain of the lack of notice and hearing
provided for in the FUTA since the state had declared a clear
legislative intent to establish a streamlined procedure to take
place prior to and outside the procedures prescribed in the
federal statute.

1-28-64 Letter, Goodwin to the Secretary, advised that a bill
(Senate Bill 179) pending in the state legislature would make
inoperative the provisions of Senate Bill 89 until June 30,
1964, and operative thereafter unless the Governor certifies
otherwise:

> WHEREAS, in order to demonstrate the good
> faith of the people of the Sovereign State of South
> Dakota, it is hereby declared the policy of the
> legislature of the State of South Dakota to make
> the provisions of Chapter 125 of the Session Laws
> of 1963 inoperative for a limited period of time in
> order to give the Secretary of Labor an opportunity
> to follow the applicable federal statutes relating to
> the conformity of State acts, thereby preserving

comity between the Sovereign State of South Dakota and the United States Government.

1-30-64 Wilkins called and reported to Norwood that the South Dakota Attorney General had ruled against the Secretary's decision because a hearing was not held.

2-3-64 Memorandum from Wilkins to Miller forwarded copies of Senate Bills 179 and 180 (a seasonality provision) as well as other bills and a news item which described State Attorney General's opinion that Secretary's "finding" was not valid since no notice was given and no hearing held. The legislature was authorized to last 30 legislative days beginning 1-7-64. More than 20 days had elapsed.

2-4-64 Altman reported to Norwood that the Regional office indicated that Senate Bills 179 and 180 had passed the State Senate, were reported favorably by the House Committee, and were expected to pass February 6. Senate Bill 180 was the seasonality provision, which provided that benefits would be paid a claimant in a calendar quarter only to the extent they could be based on the claimant's employment in the corresponding quarter of the base period. There would be no benefits paid to a claimant in the first quarter of 1964, for example, if the claimant had not worked in the first quarter of 1963. The bill would allegedly adversely affect over 40 percent of the claimants. The legislature was expected to adjourn in a few days.

2-13-64 Governor approved Senate Bill 179 providing that previously enacted Senate Bill 89, at issue, would become inoperative through June 30, 1964, but would become operative on and after July 1, 1964,

> . . . unless the Governor of the State of South Dakota on or before December 31, 1964, declares the same to be inoperative by certifying such declaration to the Secretary of State and the Commissioner and Counsel of Employment Security.

[Available record not clear as to the action at this time on Senate Bill 180. It appears, on the basis of subsequent events, that the bill was indeed enacted but never became effective because of labor's successful referendum drive and the bill's subsequent defeat at the polls, as noted in entry for 11-4-64.]

3-10-64 Governor requested Secretary, at his early convenience, to afford the state reasonable notice and opportunity to be heard, as provided in federal law.

3-30-64 Memorandum to the Secretary from Charles Donahue and Robert C. Goodwin advised that although conformity proceedings could begin before July 1, 1964 no finding could be made unless and until Senate Bill 89 should become operative. Until then the Secretary could not legally find that the state has amended its law so that it no longer contains the provisions required by the FUTA.

3-30-64 Separate letter from Goodwin to Secretary pointed out that Goodwin accepted the judgment of the Solicitor's Office that a finding could not be made prior to July 1. He indicated, however, that he was hopeful of at least a hearing before then since the Governor clearly is seeking early action; delay could cause the hearing and decision to occur during state and national political party conventions and the finding could become a campaign issue; it will be difficult to hold a hearing after July 1 and issue a decision prior to October 1, which would be necessary in order for it to become effective December 31, as required by the FUTA.

4-7-64 Memorandum from Wilkins to Miller attached copy of letter dated 4-6-64 from Yaukey to Wilkins which advised that the state law permits new laws passed by the state legislature to be considered by the voters at the election, provided appropriate petitions are filed by May 15. Letter included article from the Aberdeen *American News* which quoted Cliff Shrader, President of the South Dakota Federation of Labor, as saying that petitions to get Senate Bill 180 (seasonality provision) referred in the general election in November would be circulated throughout South Dakota.

4-29-64 Letter from the Secretary to the Governor pointed out that under federal law it would be premature to proceed with the conformity matter prior to July 1. However, as a preliminary step to a hearing, and as required by the FUTA, he notified the Governor that he had reason to believe that the state may not be certifiable for taxable year 1964.

5-12-64 Memo from Wilkins to Miller advised that the South Dakota State Federation of Labor, AFL-CIO, succeeded in getting 19,701 names on petitions although only 12,500 minimum were needed. Accordingly, Senate Bill 180 will not go into effect after June 30, irrespective of any action taken by the Governor on Senate Bill 179. The fate of Senate Bill 180 would be decided by the voters in November.

5-22-64 Internal UIS staff memo indicated it would require a minimum of 650 man-hours to research the following items in DOL files: conformity, dependents' allowances, seasonal employment, waiting period, legislation, rules and regulations.

6-9-64 Secretary letters to Governor and Maloney enclosed a notice of hearing for 10:00 a.m. on July 7, 1964 in the main labor building in Washington. Clifford P. Grant, a hearing examiner, was designated to preside over the hearing.

6-11-64 Letters from Goodwin to Congressmen Reifel and Berry of South Dakota and Senators Mundt and McGovern advised them of the notice of hearing.

6-12-64 Letter from Norwood to Maloney requested information on the number of covered workers who earned $6,000 or more over a recent 12-month period broken down by major industry groupings.

6-13-64 Notice of hearing published in the *Federal Register.*

7-6-64 Memorandum from Norwood to Goodwin advised that Georgia, Texas and Virginia had indicated their intention to send representatives to appear at the hearing, that Jeremiah Murphy will appear on behalf of the Greater South Dakota Employers' Association and that there will be a spokesman for the AFL-CIO as well as the South Dakota Federation of Labor.

7-7-64 Memorandum, Miller to all Regional Directors, enclosed a summary of the arguments presented at the hearing.

The Department argued:

(1) The provision would deny benefits on a basis other than claimants' unemployment.

(2) The basis for the denial is an income test, similar to those used in programs for the needy.

(3) Dependents' allowances do not involve a means test since they do not condition payment on base-period earnings, nor is dependency the basis for qualifying.

(4) The average claimant who earned over $6,000 would not have received any benefits for his first spell of unemployment since the disqualification period (7-13 weeks) is longer than the average spell of unemployment.

(5) As the claimant's earnings increased from $6,000 to $9,000 or more the disqualification would increase from 7 to 13 weeks and wipe out many compensated weeks in later spells of unemployment.

(6) A South Dakota agency study made in June 1964 at DOL's request shows that 81,560 workers would have met the qualifying wage requirements of the state law. The new amendment could have adversely affected the benefit rights of 16,800 or 21 percent of these workers since their earnings were $6,000 or more.

South Dakota argued:

(1) Since the Secretary had already issued an adverse finding, they did not really expect the Hearing Examiner to reverse the Secretary's findings.

(2) The state has a right to impose a delay period upon claimants following their separation from employment. States have wide latitude to adopt programs to their own circumstances.

(3) There is no specific federal requirement that benefits should be paid as a matter of right and not on a needs basis.

(4) Compliance with federal statutes need be only of a general nature, and minor specific points should be resolved in favor of the states.

(5) Many state laws treat groups of claimants differently without raising conformity issues.

(6) There is no authority for holding the South Dakota provision inconsistent on the basis of a requirement not expressly contained in federal laws but which is merely derived by "necessary implication" from such language. An administrator cannot enlarge by interpretation the regulatory power spelled out in the statute.

(7) The provision in question is not a prohibited means test because:

> (a) It does not require an examination of a claimant's present income or other resources.
>
> (b) It applies not more of a means test than does the program itself, which is based on the presumed need of the unemployed as a class.
>
> (c) It is no different in principle than dependents' allowances, or weighted benefit schedules, which vary benefit amounts according to earnings or presumed needs of recipients.

At the conclusion of the hearing, the parties of record agreed to file initial briefs within 14 days and reply briefs within 7 days thereafter. Other interested parties had a 21-day period prescribed for filing briefs in the Notice of Hearing.

7-20-64 Brief of the State of South Dakota argued that federal law requires only that money be withdrawn solely in the payment of unemployment compensation, and that the South Dakota amendment meets this requirement. The money is paid only for unemployment benefits and not for anything else. However, "because the South Dakota amendment does not square with the concepts of social thinkers in the Bureau, this 'paraphrased law,' with the aid of a strained interpretation of 'compensation,' sprinkled with a goodly amount of poetic license and academic reasoning, threatens to become a 'compliance club' held over the head of a Sovereign State."

A second point was that, like other states' provisions, the South Dakota amendment recognized "that for certain groups, presumed needs on the average were different from those of other groups and there could be a certain tailoring of the unemployment insurance theory and procedures to meet those varying presumed needs."

A third point was that the state provision did not deal with individual need, and that is all that the federal law prohibits.

7-27-64 Georgia brief's main thrust was that DOL had no statutory or judicial authority to interpret federal law beyond the specific terms of the Acts and that a "necessary implication" can arise only when there can be no other reasonable interpretation. The administrative interpretation relating to the South Dakota provision had no basis in the Act.

8-4-64 The Department of Labor's Reply Brief transmitted to Maloney by Solicitor's Office Counsel for Unemployment Compensation, Louise Freeman, argued that although South Dakota and the other states acknowledged that a means test is prohibited by federal law as inconsistent with basic unemployment insurance principles, they nevertheless argue that as long as money withdrawn from the fund is paid for the relief of unemployment, there can be no conflict with federal law. According to the Department, if the withdrawal standard was interpreted as permitting use of fund moneys for any program in relief of the unemployed, as urged by the states, it could not then be said that the federal law prohibited either a means or an income test—even though the states had agreed that it did contain such a prohibition.

8-13-64 Stanley Rector, writing in the *Advisor* (a periodical published by an organization, headed by Rector, that provided UI advice to business) disagreed with DOL and argued that the South Dakota decision (and an earlier decision concerning a New Hampshire provision) would provide the necessary momentum for a Judicial Review Bill. "There is now no semblance of due process in the procedure in which the Department of Labor is judge, jury, and executioner."

8-24-64 Recommended decision of Hearing Examiner Clifford P. Grant held that under the South Dakota provision, eligibility for benefits would be premised upon not exceeding a specified amount of income from earnings in the base period, "a condition of entitlement unrelated to the fact or cause of unemployment and therefore inconsistent with the stated requirements of the Federal law. It is difficult to understand, by any stretch of the imagination, how this contributes to the goals of economic stability and the relief of the unemployed."

> If the language of the Federal law is not in itself sufficiently plain to preclude the application to the income-from-earnings test as a condition of entitlement unrelated to the fact or cause of unemployment, one need look only to the intent of Congress and its mandate for 'genuine unemployment com-

pensation laws' for the principle that unemployment compensation is to be paid as a matter of right without any test of means or other condition of entitlement not reasonably related to the insurance program or to the insured risk, involuntary unemployment.

9-1-64 South Dakota's exception to the recommended decision of the Hearing Examiner argued that the law contemplated that the states were to be given wide latitude as long as they did not examine the poverty or need of the individual claimant or violate the few other limitations in the federal law; that other state provisions deviated from the principle that benefits must be based solely on unemployment in that they grouped claimants (Great Lakes seamen in Ohio, interstate claimants in Alaska, women, students and claimants with dependents) for reasons wholly unrelated to their unemployment and treat them differently. In each case, the specified category is singled out for special treatment: Great Lakes seamen were subject to a special seasonality provision in Ohio; interstate claimants received lower benefits than intrastate claimants under Alaska law; claimants with dependents receive special allowances in some states; women are the subject of special pregnancy and leaving work disqualifications; and students are subject to special restrictions.

9-4-64 Record of proceedings certified to Secretary of Labor by Clifford Grant.

9-25-64 Secretary's letter to Governor of South Dakota enclosed copy of Secretary's decision in which the Secretary concurred in and adopted the findings and conclusions contained in the recommended decision of the Hearing Examiner. This decision

> . . . finds that the South Dakota Employment Security Law, as amended by Chapter 125 of the

Session Laws of 1963, no longer contains the provisions specified in Section 3304(a)(4) of the Internal Revenue Code of 1954 and Section 303(a)(5) of the Social Security Act.

10-2-64 Unemployment Insurance Program Letter 787 distributed decision to all state Employment Security agencies.

11-4-64 Wilkins advised Miller that agency officials planned to meet with Governor during the week of November 16. Also, with one-half the returns counted, the referendum on Senate Bill 180 was defeated and the seasonality provision would not go into effect. South Dakota AFL-CIO had distributed 20,000 copies of "Questions and Answers on Senate Bill No. 180" throughout the state in the ten days to two weeks preceding the election and had put newspaper ads in the six leading state papers in the October 24, 27 and 31 issues.

11-16-64 Wilkins advised Miller that the Governor had declared Senate Bill 179 inoperative as of November 16, 1964.

12-11-64 Letter from Secretary acknowledged receipt of certified copy of Governor's action and advised that it constituted the necessary remedial action so that the finding of nonconformity would not be a basis for noncertification of tax credit or denial of administrative grants.

NOTES

1. This, of course, is true only of the regular unemployment insurance system. It does not apply to the two federal unemployment compensation programs for ex-servicepersons (UCX) and federal employees (UCFE). In those cases federal legislation is implemented not through state legislation, but through agreement with the states to act as agents for the federal government.

2. Where the weekly benefit amount is computed as a fraction of high quarter earnings and base-period wages must equal a multiple of the weekly benefit amount, an increase in the maximum benefit amount could result in some individuals with substantial high quarter earnings failing to meet the base-period requirements—unless the state has a "stepdown" provision. For discussion of other benefit formula inter-relationships, see U.S. Department of Labor, Bureau of Employment Security, *Unemployment Insurance Legislative Policy, Recommendations for State Legislation 1962,* BES No. U-212A, October 1962, pp. 44-50, particularly.

3. *Ibid.,* pp. 50-51.

4. *Ibid.*

5. See, for example, discussion of the "Knowland Amendment" in William Haber and Merrill G. Murray, *Unemployment Insurance in the American Economy* (Homewood, IL: Richard D. Irwin, Inc., 1966), p. 450.

6. See discussion of New Hampshire case (1980) under *Coverage Issues* in chapter 5.

7. This chronology was compiled from an examination of correspondence in the Department of Labor's South Dakota conformity files, Washington, DC.

Chapter 5
Major Federal-State Conformity and Court Cases

This nation's system of unemployment insurance would simply not survive without continuing cooperation between the federal and state partners. Mutual respect, understanding, and appreciation for each other's responsibilities are key factors in keeping the system going. But the day-to-day demonstrations of these qualities are buried and taken for granted. Rather, it is the occasional conflict that produces the drama, attention, and sometimes significant change in the program's direction.

The foregoing chapters identified two categories of conflicts. First are those that are almost constantly erupting and are not subject to permanent or complete resolution. They are the inevitable result of the division of responsibilities between two levels of government. They would not exist under either a wholly federal or a wholly state program, but they are more than offset by the advantages of the hybrid system. The other category includes conflicts over the meaning of federal law—actually over the meaning of unemployment insurance. These conflicts are usually resolved through negotiation and the informal means described in chapter 4.

The issues *not* so settled are decided in either of two ways. Increasingly, issues are resolved by federal imposition of program standards. As chapter 3 pointed out, this approach

171

is often incompatible with a program grounded on intergovernmental cooperation. Federal program standards have not only produced resentment and disruption, but in most cases their adoption has been either unnecessary or undesirable.

The other way issues have been resolved is through conformity hearings and litigation. This is not to say that conformity hearings are alternative means of settling the same issues. Federal standards create new law while conformity proceedings merely test interpretations of existing law. Still, both are means of settling issues and coping with problems.

Standards adopted in recent years have provoked resentment, undermined confidence in federal judgment, generated administrative problems and, most important, weakened the balance of power, the key to the program's success. In contrast, conformity hearings have proved to be a successful means of renewing the program. They too are accompanied by the heat of conflict. Disputes have been serious, highly controversial and often volatile struggles over basic principles. But by providing an arena for full expression of opposing views, the conformity process reveals weaknesses to be corrected. It provokes continual reexamination of original principles, and it satisfies the need of the states for their "day in court" and a fair hearing and determination of their grievance.

Every past major federal-state conflict over the meaning of federal law which went to formal hearing is described in this chapter. Aside from the 1963-1964 South Dakota case first discussed and described in chapter 4 to illustrate the process, these conflicts are grouped for convenience into four subject categories by the nature of the issues involved: administrative; coverage; experience rating and benefit charging; and labor standards. The final section in this chapter deals with fair hearing and promptness issues which were not raised in conformity actions by the federal government. They were instead brought by claimants against states and pursued through the courts. Their actions have profoundly affected the federal-state system.

South Dakota (1963-64) Issues

The South Dakota case was the most important of all conformity cases so far and one of the few that involved more than a single issue. There were four. The most prominent was whether the state's variable waiting period keyed to the level of base-period wage earnings constituted a prohibited income test. The problem with the state provision was that, among otherwise equally eligible claimants, payment or denial would be conditioned on a factor (variation in base-period earnings) bearing absolutely no relationship to unemployment. This violated one of the most significant interpretations of two federal provisions: that money withdrawn from the fund may be used only for unemployment compensation, and that "compensation" means benefits payable to individuals with respect to their unemployment. The decision was that the federal law provisions preclude not only a clear-cut needs test as a condition for benefits, but also an income test of the type enacted by South Dakota.

The second issue concerned the extent of federal authority to interpret federal laws. The state had argued that only requirements expressly contained in the statutes were binding and DOL had no statutory or judicial authority to interpret beyond the specific terms of the Acts. DOL could only draw necessary implications, and these arise only when there can be no other reasonable interpretation. A decision in favor of the state on this issue would have resulted in a substantial realignment of federal-state authority. Many conformity issues, particularly experience rating issues, are provoked by interpretations considerably more fragile than DOL's construction of the federal requirement that money withdrawn from the fund must be used only for unemployment compensation. The issue was not really joined at the hearing except that once the state had acknowledged, as it did, that an individual needs test was inconsistent with federal law, DOL pointed out that since the law did not contain an explicit prohibition, the state's conclusion, with which it agreed, could be reached only by reasonable interpretation.

The third issue was also raised in two subsequent conformity cases. The states involved contended that federal law did not contemplate application of the awesome sanctions (total loss of federal tax credit and administrative grants) for minor violations. It was wholly unreasonable, they argued, for a provision affecting a relatively small handful of claimants to incur a penalty threatening the continued existence of the state's program. It was enough for a state to conform substantially with the federal requirements.

However, the language of the law is in absolute terms. It requires, as a condition for tax credit and administrative grants, that the state law "shall provide," with no allowance for deviation. Acceptance of the state argument would, in addition, invite endless debate over the meaning of "substantial" in individual cases, and it is for this reason that DOL has consistently rejected the *de minimus* argument. The South Dakota hearing was no exception.

The last issue concerned the fairness of the proceeding. The states had argued that they were disadvantaged by a process under which only the Department of Labor challenges and judges the conformity of the state law, and because the hearing is held in Washington, before an administrative law judge appointed by the Secretary of Labor, with the issue finally determined by the same Secretary of Labor. The Department did not answer these allegations at the hearing, but it did not object to a provision, included in the 1970 amendments (P.L. 91-373), establishing a state's right to judicial review of an adverse Secretary's decision.

Administrative Issues

The first two issues in this category concerned violation of an explicit federal provision (payment only through public employment offices or such other agencies as the Board may approve), and interpretation of the requirement that administrative grants may be used only for purposes found by the Secretary to be necessary for proper and efficient administration. The third concerned interpretation of the "methods of administration" requirement and the provision restricting the use of money withdrawn from the fund to unemployment compensation purposes. This case, suspended indefinitely, demonstrated that there are limits to interpretation, even of the most ambiguous (methods of administration) federal requirements.

South Dakota (1939)

In early 1939, the state legislature adjourned without appropriating any funds to match (as was then required by the Wagner-Peyser Act) federal grants for the employment services. The state proposed to pay UI benefits through the state welfare offices instead of employment offices. Provisions of the FUTA and the Social Security Act require state laws to provide payment of benefits only through public employment offices·or such other agencies as the Social Security Board (now Secretary of Labor) may approve.[1] The Board had not approved welfare offices for this purpose and therefore federal UI administrative grants were withheld. Subsequently, the state provided the necessary money and public employment offices were reopened in September when grants were resumed. By the time of year-end certification for the federal tax credit, the state program was in conformity.

Arizona (1941)

In January 1941, the Arizona Unemployment Compensation Commission abolished the position of Executive Director, which was included in the state's merit system, and discharged its incumbent. On June 2, 1941, the state Supreme Court held that the incumbent had been illegally released by the Commission and ordered him reinstated with back pay. He was reinstated June 5, 1941 and held his position until June 15, 1941, when an amendment to the state UI law designating the Director of the state Employment Service as Executive Director of the entire agency became effective, thus legally removing the previous director.

The issue was whether administrative grants could be used to pay the salary of the former Executive Director during the period he rendered no service to the agency.[2] The Social Security Board concluded that the Commission had not acted in good faith and, therefore, the salary payments could not be considered necessary for proper and efficient administration.

New Hampshire (1964)

The issue in this case concerned a state practice in which, on request by the attorney who represented a claimant in a successful court appeal on the claimant's right to benefits, the agency sent the claimant's benefit checks to the attorney. The agency considered this tantamount to delivery to the claimant. The question was whether the state law, as so interpreted by the agency, violated provisions of the FUTA and Social Security Act[3] which require that all money withdrawn from the state's unemployment fund may be used only for payment of unemployment compensation. Another question was whether the practice violated the Social Security Act requirement[4] that the state law provide methods of administration reasonably calculated to ensure full payment of benefits when due.

At a conformity hearing held by DOL in May 1964, six other states appeared or filed briefs indicating that they too mailed checks to persons other than the beneficiary under certain circumstances. In July 1964, the Secretary of Labor dismissed the proceedings and directed the Department's Bureau of Employment Security to review various state practices and recommend an appropriate standard. No standard was ever issued because of the failure of the Bureau and the Office of the Solicitor to agree on its content, and the practice continues.

Coverage Issues

State law coverage of certain employing units was made a matter of conformity for the first time in 1970 by the employment security amendments enacted that year (P.L. 91-373). All coverage prior to that time, and some coverage since, was effected by making specified services subject to the federal tax. States invariably extended coverage to the same services in order to permit the newly covered employers to enjoy the credit against the federal tax, to ensure that the bulk of the employers' unemployment insurance taxes would be paid to the state, and to extend the protection of the program to those performing the newly covered services. A state that did not provide coverage at least as extensive as under the federal law would forfeit these advantages with respect to the specific employers and workers, but such failure would not present an issue of conformity with federal law. The 1970 amendments, however, required, as a condition for tax credit for *all* a state's employers, that state law cover certain nonprofit organizations and state hospitals and institutions of higher education. This approach was taken because these employers were not subject to the federal UI tax and therefore were not affected by loss of tax offset for failure to cover them. Required coverage was similarly extended by the 1976 amendments to most services performed by employees for state and local governments. All the coverage issues to date arise under either the 1970 or 1976 amendments.

New York (1974)

The 1970 amendments added a provision in the FUTA[5] to require state coverage of employment by nonprofit organizations and state hospitals and institutions of higher education. The FUTA was also amended to prohibit the Secretary of Labor from certifying any state he finds,

> . . . after reasonable notice and opportunity for hearing . . . has failed to amend its law so that it contains each of the provisions required by reason of the enactment of the Employment Security Amendments of 1970 to be included therein, or has . . . failed to comply substantially with any such provision.[6]

The State of New York, in amending its law to effect the necessary coverage, deliberately retained the following exclusions from the definition of "employment":

(1) golf caddies;
(2) students in elementary or secondary schools who work part-time during the school year or regular vacation periods;
(3) minors engaged in casual labor consisting of yard work and household chores not involving the use of power driven machinery;
(4) all employment performed by persons under 14 years of age.

However, there were no comparable exclusions in the federal law definition of "employment" contained in the FUTA.[7] Nor were the services among those specified in the FUTA that a state was permitted to exclude from the otherwise required coverage.[8] The New York law was challenged and a hearing was held on August 7, 1974. The Administrative Law Judge issued a Recommended Decision on November 11, 1974, and the Secretary of Labor issued his decision on June 6, 1975 holding the law out of conformity.

New York offered two arguments. First, it pointed out that the exclusions from the state's definition of "employment" apply equally to profit, nonprofit, and state institutions. It then argued that the 1970 provision added to the FUTA required only that coverage for service performed for nonprofit organizations, state hospitals and state institutions of higher education be co-extensive with the coverage the state requires for service performed for all other employers. This conclusion was based on the following "equal treatment" requirement of the FUTA provision that state laws provide that:

> . . . compensation is payable on the basis of service to which Section 3309(a)(1) applies [nonprofits and State hospitals and institutions of high education] in the same amount, on the same terms, and subject to the same conditions as compensation payable on the basis of other service subject to such law. . . .[9]

Since profit making enterprises, the state's institutions, and nonprofit organizations were all subject to the New York exclusions, the state argued that such even-handedness satisfied the "equal treatment" requirement and, accordingly, the coverage requirement. In other words, New York interpreted the federal law as permitting certain services performed for nonprofits and state institutions to be exempt from coverage, if the same services are also excluded when performed for profit making employers.

The argument was rejected on the grounds that the "equal treatment" requirement merely describes the manner in which benefits are to be administratively dispensed. According to the Secretary's decision,

> It does not follow that a provision which deals with terms and conditions of compensation can be cited as justification for eliminating categories of coverage. . . .[10]

On the contrary,

> The whole thrust of Congressional intent was the extension of coverage, and the limitation of exceptions to the new coverage. . . . The only exceptions to coverage which may properly be applied, and the only persons (or categories of persons) who may properly be excluded from coverage, are those which are set forth in the Federal statute. To allow otherwise is to fly in the face of the 1970 Amendments. Congress can hardly be deemed to have engaged in a self-defeating exercise by, on the one hand, providing for the extension of coverage, and, on the other hand, allowing the States to carve out exceptions to the new coverage as the States see fit.[11]

New York's second argument concerned the nature of the exclusions in question. The state argued that since few or none of the excluded individuals work for nonprofit organizations or state hospitals or institutions of higher education, the whole affair was *de minimus.* Substantial compliance of its legislation with the 1970 Amendments was really all that is required. Minor deviations should be permissible. This argument also was rejected:

> Statutorily, there is no provision allowing mere 'substantial compliance' of the State law with FUTA requirements placed upon the law, itself. Substantive compliance is relevant only to the operation of the State under its law. Nor is 'substantial compliance' in the operation of its law some sort of substitute for conformity of the State law with the Federal statutory mandate. If the State law has not been amended to contain each of the provisions required by reason of the 1970 Amendments, it cannot, by terms of 26 U.S.C. 3304(c), be certified by the Secretary.[12]

The issue was important, particularly in light of the later substantive extensions of required coverage under the 1976 Amendments. If New York had prevailed on the basis of its first argument, there would have been doubt as to the extent of DOL's authority to require coverage of any category of state, local or nonprofit occupation, if the state excluded corresponding occupations in the private-for-profit sector. If the *de minimus* argument had prevailed, DOL would have faced the difficult task of establishing reliable criteria for determining when a violation was too minor to pursue.

Pennsylvania (1979)

A conformity hearing was held with Pennsylvania August 21, 1979 on three separate issues. One is discussed below as an experience rating issue. The remaining two issues involved provisions of the 1976 Amendments extending coverage to school employees. Under these amendments, the federal law prohibits states from paying benefits, based on services performed in an instructional, research or principal administrative capacity for an educational institution during the period between school terms if the individual performed such services during the first term and had a reasonable assurance of performing similar services during the suc-

ceeding term.[13] States had the option of applying the same
between-terms denial provisions to nonprofessional primary
and secondary school employees. Aside from this exception,
federal law required states to provide governmental and nonprofit employees the same treatment as applied to other
covered workers.

Pennsylvania had adopted the option of applying the
between-terms denial provisions to nonprofessional
employees, but it included a unique provision. An individual, denied benefits during the summer school break
because of a reasonable assurance of reemployment the
following term, could collect benefits for the summer period
retroactively,

> . . . if upon presenting himself for work at the end
> of such period between academic years or terms,
> the individual is not permitted to resume work of
> the same capacity, or resumes it for less than twen-
> ty working days. . . .[14]

Pennsylvania argued that its law could be denied certification only if it plainly conflicts with the FUTA. Also, it questioned DOL's authority to impose on a state its interpretation of the FUTA as a matter of conformity. The Secretary
of Labor rejected both contentions and ruled on October 31,
1979 in support of the Administrative Law Judge's conclusion that the retroactive provision conflicted with the FUTA.
The basis for that conclusion was that federal law prohibited
payment between terms to an individual who had bona fide
reasonable assurance of returning to work, regardless of
whether the job actually materialized. The provision also
violated the "equal treatment" requirement since no other
category of workers was offered the opportunity for retroactive benefits. Finally, the Department pointed out that in
enacting the 1976 Amendments providing for the coverage of
primary and secondary school employees and the benefit

restrictions, Congress rejected an amendment providing a retroactive benefit provision similar to Pennsylvania's.

The second issue also involved the between-terms denial provisions, which apply to persons performing specified services "for an educational institution" or persons performing such services, "in an educational institution while in the employ of an educational service agency." Educational service agencies are defined as "a governmental agency or governmental entity which is established and operated exclusively for the purpose of providing such services to one or more educational institutions. . . ."[15] Pennsylvania interpreted its law to apply the between-terms denial to school crossing guards and others who are not employed directly by either an educational institution or an educational service agency, but who perform services for schools and whose employment is tied to the academic calendar. The Department argued that the phrase "for an educational institution" was intended to mean only individuals actually employed by a school, or an educational service agency, not school crossing guards if employed by the police department or other agency. It pointed out that the Congress evidently shared that view because, prior to the specific amendment,[16] not even employees of educational service agencies were considered within the scope of the between-terms denial. If the phrase "for an educational institution" had been intended to apply to individuals other than actual school employees, the later amendment would not have been necessary. The between-terms denial was intended to be a limited exception to the equal treatment requirement. The Department argued that in extending the denial to nonemployees of schools (or educational service agencies), Pennsylvania violated the equal treatment requirement.

Pennsylvania argued that the between-terms denial provision as it applies to nonemployees of schools should be disregarded, since under another section of the Pennsylvania law municipal employees such as school crossing guards are denied benefits anyway, as not available for suitable work. The Administrative Law Judge rejected this argument and held that what the state's availability requirement provides was irrelevant and that the Pennsylvania between-terms provision, as interpreted by the agency, was inconsistent with federal law. The Secretary adopted this position.

New Hampshire (1980)

In 1978, the New Hampshire legislature passed legislation intended to meet the coverage and the requirements of P.L. 94-566, the 1976 amendment. The bill was vetoed by Governor Meldrim Thomson. The Governor and the state agency argued that the federal law requirements represented an improper intrusion upon the state's sovereignty and were thus unconstitutional:

> Is there not to be some time, some place, some one who will say that the sovereign rights reserved to this state by our Founding Fathers are an integral part of our constitutional fabric and cannot be ripped asunder by a power-crazed Federal Government.[17]

On October 30, 1978, after a conformity hearing, the Secretary of Labor found that the New Hampshire law failed to conform to FUTA requirements for certification. The actual withdrawal of certification was held in abeyance pending outcome of the state's appeal to the courts. Of the following six issues, the most important involves the state's failure to extend coverage to the extent required by the FUTA as a condition for certification.

(1) The state law excluded service performed for political subdivisions from coverage as well as service performed for the state by individuals not on the state classified ser-

vice and not employees of state hospitals and institutions of higher education.

(2) The state also excluded employees of nonprofit elementary and secondary schools.

(3) No provision was included permitting governmental entities to elect either the tax or reimbursement method of financing benefit costs.

(4) The state's language concerning the denial of benefits to uncertified aliens differed considerably from the FUTA requirement.

(5) Similarly, the state's language concerning denial of benefits during the off-season to professional athletes also differed from the corresponding FUTA requirement.

(6) The state's between-terms denial provisions applied to nonprofessional employees of colleges and universities, inconsistently with the FUTA.

At the conformity hearing held in September 1978, the New Hampshire agency contended that the federal statute is not phrased in absolute terms and that substantive compliance with federal law is sufficient to avoid withholding of certification. The agency argued also that because of New Hampshire's unique base period and benefit year,[18] no benefits based on 1978 wages would be payable before April 1, 1979, so the hearing was premature. The Secretary rejected both contentions on the grounds that the FUTA prohibits certification under either of two conditions: either the state law fails to contain certain required provisions, or the state has failed to comply substantially with any such provision during the 12-month period.[19] The first condition requires strict conformity between the state law and the FUTA. Substantive compliance assumes the existence of conforming state law provisions and is aimed at their administration. All the issues involved the conformity of the state law, not the manner of its administration. Accordingly, the concept of substantial compliance was not at issue, and the fact that no New Hampshire claimant may yet have been deprived of benefits was immaterial. The state also raised constitutional issues concerning the FUTA requirement for state coverage of services performed for the state and its political subdivisions. Neither the Administrative Law Judge nor the Secretary ruled on the constitutionality of the federal statute.

The Secretary's 1978 decision was appealed by New Hampshire to the United States Court of Appeals for the First Circuit, which stayed the Secretary's decision pending outcome of the appeal.

While the 1978 case was pending before the Court of Appeals, newly elected Governor Hugh Gallen who took office in January 1979 requested later that year that the Court postpone issuing a decision pending a possible settlement of the case. The Court agreed. Efforts were made to develop a compromise under which the state would by statute, regulations, and Attorney General opinion, effect conformity with the federal requirements, both prospectively and retrospectively. However, the Commissioner of the State Department of Employment Security (DES), which had autonomous status independent of the Governor, and his counsel refused either to sign a consent decree to which the Departments of Labor and Justice and the State Attorney General had agreed or to take the administrative actions DOL believed necessary to correct the damage done by the failure of the state to conform. On February 20, 1980, the U.S. Court of Appeals for the First Circuit decided in favor of DOL on all issues.[20]

The state filed a further appeal in May 1980 to the U.S. Supreme Court. The Court, treating the appeal as a petition for certiorari, denied further review on October 6, 1980. On

October 28, 1980, Secretary Marshall advised Governor
Gallen that,

> I believe at this point that there is no alternative
> under the law other than to withhold the certifica-
> tions which would result in the loss by New Hamp-
> shire employers of the credits taken tentatively by
> them for taxable year 1978 under Section 3302 of
> the Code, and to recoup the administrative grants
> provided for that year. If you have any information
> that may be pertinent to the decision I feel I must
> make, please let me know as soon as possible.

A response dated the following day from Governor Gallen
requested that the Secretary meet with the Governor and the
State Attorney General before actually decertifying the state
and sending notification of that action to the Treasury
Department. The Governor pointed out that although his administration, the Attorney General, the state legislature and
the business community believed the state should have conformed to the federal law, this was prevented by Governor
Thomson's 1978 veto and the DES Commissioner's steadfast
refusal to settle the lawsuit. The Governor explained that
since the U.S. Supreme Court decision, he had issued an
Executive Order transferring all of the agency's attorneys to
the Office of the Attorney General and that he believed that
he now had adequate authority to bring the state into conformity.

On December 18, 1980, Governor Gallen wrote to the
Secretary advising him of his understanding, from the
Justice Department's Tax Division and from a Congressional Research Service legal memorandum, that the
Secretary has authority under the law to certify New Hampshire retroactively for 1978 and to decline to impose any
sanctions. The Governor argued that the disastrous consequences to the New Hampshire community of imposing the

sanctions far outweighed the effect they would have of deter-
ring other states from availing themselves of judicial review.

> The sanctions themselves are not graded in any way
> to take into account the intent or the actions of the
> State that suffers them. Beyond that, as you know,
> they are imposed on members of the private
> business community who are not parties to con-
> troversies such as this, whose decisions could not
> have affected the outcome, and who are innocent
> of any wrongdoing. In this case we have lost at
> every stage of the administrative and judicial pro-
> ceedings, we have taken steps to conform our law
> in every material respect for 1978, and have stood
> willing for weeks now to do anything else which
> may be required to meet both in law and in fact
> your standard of conformity. I do not see how our
> experience could conceivably encourage any other
> jurisdiction to take the same course. Under these
> circumstances your interest in deterrence has been
> more than adequately served.

On January 19, 1981, Secretary Marshall advised Governor
Gallen of his decision to certify the State of New Hampshire
for the 12-month period ending October 31, 1978, conditioned upon the state's compliance with an agreement signed the
same day by both parties. First, the state (whose law was certified for 1980 after including necessary rules, regulations
and Attorney General's opinions) was to apply the conforming provisions retroactively to January 1, 1978, to accomplish substantial compliance with respect to the six issues
in question. The state was required also to make certain
reports concerning its compliance action. In addition, the
state was to repay in six installments to the Department of
Labor $3.3 million representing the grant to the state for ad-
ministration of its unemployment insurance program in
1978. If, however, the Secretary determined that the state

had taken all required action on or before October 31, 1981, he would reduce the amount due to $500,000 payable on or before December 31, 1981. It is not clear how this figure was determined. It may represent one of the six installments. When the amount due DOL had been paid, the state's certification would become final. If the state legislature failed to appropriate the money for the payment due, the certification for 1979 would be withheld.

There were also conformity issues raised formally with respect to the state's 1979 law. New Hampshire amended its unemployment compensation law in June 1979 to meet the federal requirements of the 1976 amendments. It did so reluctantly: "Wherefor, the legislature having no alternative but to accede to this federal intrusion of its State sovereignty, acting under duress and for no other reason enacts this Chapter."[21] However, DOL advised the state that the amendments did not resolve all the issues and initiated a new conformity proceeding to determine certification of the state for the 12 months ending October 31, 1979. A hearing was held on September 6 and 7, 1979. On October 15, 1979, the Administrative Law Judge issued a recommended decision finding the state law not in conformity or substantial compliance with respect to seven issues. These were not significantly different from the 1978 issues. This decision was adopted by Secretary Marshall October 31, 1979.

This 1979 decision, which the state had appealed to the U.S. Court of Appeals for the First Circuit but which was held in abeyance pending possible settlement by the parties, was settled in early January 1981, by a consent judgment, subject to approval by the Court. That settlement included retroactive application of the conforming provisions to January 1, 1978, as described above. The state was directed to redetermine the claims of all individuals denied benefits under nonconforming law, including not only claimants determined ineligible under prior law but also all individuals who would have been eligible except for such law. The Court entered the consent judgment January 26, 1981. On April 6, 1981, Secretary of Labor Donovan certified the State of New Hampshire for the 12-month period ending October 31, 1979.

The importance of the New Hampshire case lies more in its implications for the conformity and judicial review processes than in the nature of the specific issues. These conformity and judicial review issues are discussed below in connection with the County of Los Angeles case. The questions the New Hampshire case raise include whether a stay of a Secretary's decision pending judicial review is equitable to those affected adversely by the state provision in question; whether fear of the consequences of a negative decision by the Courts (and consequent imposition of sanctions) will deter states from seeking judicial review; whether the sanction imposed on New Hampsire ($500,000 instead of the possible $35-$45 million loss the state would have incurred if the tax credit and administrative grants for 1978 had been denied) will encourage more states to try the conformity route rather than attempt settlement through negotiation; whether the availability of a "lesser sanction" will incline DOL to move toward hearings more quickly and on more issues than before instead of pressing for settlement through negotiation. It does not seem appropriate to speculate here on these issues, but it is pertinent to point out that the New Hampshire case could change significantly the way conformity issues are handled and, consequently, the climate of future federal-state relations.

Constitutionality Challenge: The County of Los Angeles Case (1980)

After the 1976 federal employment security amendments were enacted, but before state implementation was required, the Executive Committee of the National Institute of

Municipal Law Officers (NIMLO) sent a memorandum (March 22, 1977) to its member attorneys, in which it proposed a lawsuit attacking the constitutionality of the new coverage requirements that applied to employment by state and local governments. The Executive Committee of NIMLO described the impact of the resulting unemployment insurance costs that the new required coverage would have on state and local governments, contending that the ensuing financial drain would necessitate the reduction of public services, additional taxes and, most ironically, the separation of workers. The Executive Committee explained that the proposed action would not be brought in NIMLO's name but rather would be a multiparty suit, naming as plaintiffs "those state and local governments which decide to participate in and finance the costs of this litigation." The suit would seek relief only for plaintiffs named in the complaint and "only those state and local governments willing to help bear the costs of this litigation will be named as Plaintiffs."

Hope for success was based largely on the June 24, 1976 decision of the U.S. Supreme Court in *National League of Cities, et al.* v. *Usery, Secretary of Labor.*[22] This case involved a 1974 amendment extending application of the Fair Labor Standards Act's minimum wage and maximum hour provisions to almost all employees of states and their political subdivisions. According to Justice Rehnquist, writing for a 5-4 majority, both the minimum wage and the maximum hour provisions "will impermissibly interfere with the integral governmental functions of these bodies." The basis for this opinion was the anticipated massive impact of the requirements on the states, in terms of increased costs and reduced control over the conditions of employment of their workers. Estimates by a number of states and cities convinced the Court that "Judged solely in terms of increased costs in dollars, these allegations show a significant impact on the functioning of the governmental bodies involved.'' The same legal firm that successfully represented local governments in *National League of Cities* was hired for the County of Los Angeles suit.

Optimism also rested on a legal opinion obtained from a Wisconsin law firm, as requested by the National Association of Counties. The opinion concluded that the state and local government UI coverage requirement constituted an ''unconstitutional condition imposed upon the several States by Congress.'' The states have no realistic choice in enacting required legislation; no federal funds are provided so state and local taxes must be raised; the interest of the states with respect to the necessary funding needed to comply, together with the resulting disruption of traditional state and local employment practices, transcends the national interest presented. According to the opinion, any court battle over constitutionality would be won or lost on the basis of sufficient statistics showing (1) the impact of the cost of coverage (allegedly $500 million annually) to the states and local units of government, and (2) the measures necessary to meet the costs, which would result in ''a marked disruption'' in the employment practices of local government.

> The time appears to be appropriate to test to what degree Congress may wield its spending power to impinge upon the operation of State and local government. Based upon the balancing test applied by the Court in the *National League of Cities* case, we are inclined to believe that the scales would be tipped by the present Supreme Court in the direction of protecting the employment interests of State and local government.[23]

In August 1977, members of the International Personnel Management Association received a letter from the law firm retained by NIMLO requesting data showing the impact of the coverage requirements. According to the law firm, the case could be won

> . . . only upon a compelling presentation of the facts demonstrating the grossly burdensome and disruptive impact of the 1976 FUTA Amendments upon each Plaintiff Government.[24]

During 1977 most states enacted legislation designed to conform with the 1976 Amendments. Almost half the states included "self-destruct" provisions nullifying the extensions of coverage to states and local government workers if, in some states, the requirement was stayed by a U.S. Court or, in others, was declared constitutionally invalid in a final adjudication.

By the time the suit was heard (December 1977), the plaintiffs included the States of Alaska, South Carolina, Missouri, Nebraska, New Hampshire, New Mexico, and Utah, and 1,750 localities in 44 states. The plaintiffs, identified as the County of Los Angeles, et al., first moved for a preliminary injunction in 1977 before the United States District Court for the District of Columbia. The purpose alleged by the plaintiffs was to delay implementation of the coverage requirements so as to prevent the need for some states and localities (with constitutional or statutory limits on new debts and taxes) to curtail government services or fire employees in order to raise money for unemployment insurance costs.

District Judge Charles R. Richey denied the motion for injunction in an opinion issued December 29, 1977. He advised first that the Anti-Injunction Act appeared to bar the suit:

> No suit for the purpose of restraining the assessment or collection of any tax shall be maintained in any court by any person, whether or not such per-

son is the person against whom such tax was assessed.[25]

According to Judge Richey, since the refusal of a state to
enact the conforming legislation would result in denial of a
credit to private employers against their federal tax, the
plaintiffs' suit to prevent this denial "is in essence a suit to
restrain the assessment of a tax." Although having found it
unlikely that the Court even has jurisdiction, Judge Richey
went on to discuss the four factors a Court must consider in
deciding whether to issue any injunction:

> . . . has the plaintiff made a strong showing that it
> is likely to prevail on the merits; would the denial
> of the injunction cause irreparable injury to the
> plaintiff; would the granting of the injunction
> cause irreparable injury to the other parties; and
> where does the public interest lie.[26]

With regard to the first factor, the Court found it unlikely
that the plaintiffs would prevail on the merits. Noting that
the plaintiffs placed chief reliance on the 1977 *National
League of Cities* case decision, Judge Richey pointed out
that the regulations there concerning wage and hour standards were mandatory. The only discretion left to the states
in that instance was how to raise the additional revenue.
Citing *Steward Machine Co.* v. *Davis,*[27] the Court stated that
the imposition of an unemployment insurance scheme is at
the option of the state. By allowing the states a choice, it is
actually supportive of the Tenth Amendment. Referring to
the plaintiffs' contention that *Steward* was distinguishable
because the Supreme Court there stated that the states did
not complain of coercion, the Judge pointed out that the fact
that a state chooses to voice objection rather than remain
silent while a private employer voices objection, as in
Steward, should not be determinative of the outcome. The
same signs of coercion that were alleged in *Steward* exist

here. At the time that case was decided, 35 of the 43 states that had enacted conforming legislation included the same kind of self-destruct clauses that several states had recently enacted. "This was not enough to prove coercion in *Steward* and it is not enough now."

Concerning the second factor cited by Richey, the Court found also that the plaintiffs could avoid any alleged irreparable injury by not enacting the conforming legislation. Even if the sanctions were imposed, the state would not have to fire anyone or curtail any services. The states face no imminent injury. Judicial review of a Secretary's decision is available.

As for the last two factors cited, the Court held that the issuance of an injunction would, however, deny benefits to public employees and would thereby "cause a substantial irreparable injury to the defendants' interest and the public interest."

The decision of the U.S. Court of Appeals for the District of Columbia Circuit was issued March 19, 1980, almost a year after the appeal had been argued before the Court. The Court ruled that it had awaited the February 20, 1980 decision of the U.S. Court of Appeals for the First Circuit in the *New Hampshire* case, since the same constitutional challenge had been made by that state's Department of Employment Security: "in the interest of inter-circuit comity and the concomitant husbanding of scarce judicial resources. . . ."

> In addition to sustaining the Secretary's decertification of New Hampshire as not conforming in certain respects with FUTA, the First Circuit addressed the Tenth Amendment contention and concluded that it was unavailing. We agree with the constitutional determination so made by the First Circuit, and adopt its reasoning as fully applicable to the consolidated appeals before us.[28]

The Court briefly reiterated the mandatory versus voluntary distinctions drawn between the *National League of Cities* and the *Steward Machine Co.* cases. The District Court's dismissal of the case was affirmed. On October 6, 1980, the U.S. Supreme Court let stand the lower Court's decision.

The decision of the U.S. Court of Appeals for the First Circuit in the *New Hampshire* case was thus controlling also in the *County of Los Angeles* case. For this reason it is useful to review the *New Hampshire* case. The First Circuit Court ruled on both conformity and constitutional issues. In each of the six issues, the Court found the state law contrary to the federal law requirements and the Secretary's determination of nonconformity correct.[29] The constitutional issue boiled down to:

> . . . do the 1976 amendments to FUTA violate the sovereign integrity of the states and impair their ability to function effectively under the federal system as guaranteed by the Tenth Amendment.

The Court first distinguished the case from the *National League of Cities* case in which the issue was whether mandated application of the minimum wage and maximum hour provisions of the Fair Labor Standards Act constituted coercion of the states in contravention of the Tenth Amendment. The Act required all states to pay the majority of their workers the minimum wage rates determined by Congress. It provided for both civil and criminal penalties in the event of a violation.

The unemployment insurance amendments, based on the taxing power rather than the commerce clause, offered the states a choice of conforming or not. The petitioners argued that the option not to conform is illusory, since the severe financial consequences that would follow negate any real choice. According to the Court, however,

We do not agree that the carrot has become a club because rewards for conforming have increased. It is not the size of the stakes that controls, but the rules of the game.

In a footnote the Court noted that New Hampshire was the only state that had opted not to conform, and that it repeatedly stressed in its brief the burden on the state's employers if the Act is held constitutional. According to the Court, "We observe that it is easy to gamble for high stakes when the money on the table comes from someone else's pocket."

The Court noted that the basic design and mechanism of the federal unemployment insurance laws have not changed since 1935; coverage has been extended but the percentage of tax credit remains essentially the same. Moreover, the concept that unemployment is a national program that must be dealt with on a national basis has been woven into the fabric of our society since 1935. Accordingly, the Court ruled that the arguments of coercion that had prevailed in the *National League of Cities* case were not applicable to the 1976 amendments.

The next issue concerned the degree, if any, to which the amendments impaired New Hampshire's sovereignty, due to the cost of extending coverage to public employees. The Court noted substantial differences between the estimates of costs of the state's expert ($1.1 million) and by DOL's expert ($227,585 for fiscal 1978, $288,935 for fiscal 1979). In the *National League of Cities* case the Supreme Court found that application to states and their political subdivisions of the Fair Labor Standards Act would significantly alter or displace the ability of those governments to structure employer-employee relationships. The First Circuit Court concluded that extending UI coverage to the employees of

New Hampshire and its political subdivisions would not produce the same result:

> FUTA does not set the wage rates or affect hours worked. All it does is insure unemployment benefits for State employees. Its administration is entirely within the control of the State.

The Court held that the 1976 amendments do not impair New Hampshire's sovereignty and have not been rendered unconstitutional by reason of *National League of Cities.*

Alabama, Nevada (1981)

One of the most contentious issues arising from the 1976 amendments concerning coverage involved a question of congressional intent. Nothing in the legislative history of those amendments indicated whether, in extending coverage to employees of nonprofit primary and secondary schools, Congress intended also to cover church-related schools. The intent was ambiguous because of the manner in which coverage was affected. Prior to 1976, the FUTA included the following services performed for nonprofit organizations among those that states were permitted to exclude without jeopardizing tax credit:

> (1) in the employ of (A) a church or convention or association of churches, or (B) an organization which is operated primarily for religious purposes and which is operated, supervised, controlled or principally supported by a church or convention or association of churches;

> (2) by a duly ordained, commissioned or licensed minister of a church in the exercise of his ministry or by a member of a religious order in the exercise of duties required by such order;

(3) in the employ of a school which is not an institution of higher education.[30]

The 1976 amendments deleted paragraph (3). DOL took the position that by deleting the school exclusion, Congress intended to extend coverage to all such schools, including church-related primary and secondary schools. In following DOL's ruling, Alabama attempted to provide coverage of such schools, but was enjoined by suits filed by Baptist and Methodist churches and later enjoined permanently on January 29, 1979, by a state circuit court in a suit filed by Trinity Evangelical Lutheran Church.[31] The state voluntarily ceased its efforts to cover church-related schools.

The issue arose in Nevada because the state determined that Roman Catholic elementary and secondary schools were exempt under the state law in that services in those schools were performed in the employ of a church or a church-controlled organization operated primarily for religious purposes. Alabama and Nevada were not alone. Conformity proceedings were started by DOL against four additional states—Michigan, Tennessee, Texas and Washington. Following contentions by the four states that they had not had sufficient time to prepare for a hearing, the Secretary of Labor offered all six states certification of their laws for tax credit for 1979 and renewal of proceedings before certification was due for 1980. Alabama and Nevada alone decided to pursue the issue without further delay.

Following a conformity hearing on the Alabama and Nevada positions, held on September 26, 1979, the Administrative Law Judge (ALJ) issued his findings on October 11, 1979, recommending that the Secretary hold Alabama and Nevada in compliance with the FUTA. The ALJ agreed with the states that

> . . . church schools, being an integral part of the governing church and fundamentally religious in

character, are exempt from coverage under the plain language of Section 3309(b)(1)(A) and/or (B).

The ALJ found persuasive three lower court decisions[32] which rejected the DOL position as "contrary to the plain meaning of the statute, unsupported by the legislative history and constitutionally impermissible." He disagreed with the DOL interpretation of the language "in the employ of a church" as meaning in the employ of a house of worship, performing religious duties, and with the Department's rejection of the contention that church-schools were "operated primarily for religious purposes," rather than educational purposes.

In a decision issued October 31, 1979, Secretary of Labor Marshall rejected the ALJ's recommendation and found that the Alabama and Nevada laws failed to conform with the FUTA. The Secretary's decision referred to the fact that since the original enactment of the program, "Congress has followed an unbroken path towards expansions of unemployment insurance coverage." In extending coverage to nonprofit organizations in 1970, Congress excluded employees of primary and secondary schools, but clearly required coverage of employees of nonprofit colleges and universities, including church-related institutions of higher education, except seminaries and novitiates. In enacting the Special Unemployment Assistance Program (SUA) in 1974[33] Congress provided emergency benefit protection to unemployed workers not otherwise covered under state UI laws, including employees of church-related schools. The 1976 amendments were designed to "eliminate the temporary Special Unemployment Assistance Program" and extend "permanent" coverage to "substantially all the workers . . . covered by SUA.[34] According to the Secretary, congressional intent was indicated in a Senate Report estimating the number of employees who would be covered by eliminating the primary and secondary school exclusion as 242,000.[35] The figure, supplied to Congress by DOL, represented the total number of employees in all nonprofit primary and secondary schools of which church-related school employees represent more than half. Finally, the Secretary's decision argued that coverage of these schools did not create excessive governmental entanglement with religion and was within the limits of government regulation provided by the Constitution.

Alabama and Nevada appealed the Secretary's decision to the United States Court of Appeals for the Fifth Circuit. In September 1980, the Court reversed the Secretary's determination that the two states' laws conflicted with the FUTA. The Court supported the states' argument that church-related schools are within the statute's meaning of "church":

> . . . many of the church schools have no separate legal existence from their church; the school employees are hired, controlled, disciplined, and fired by church representatives and officials; school buildings are owned by the church; and school employees are paid with funds drawn from the church accounts.[36]

According to the Court, the exemption is contingent upon whether the workers are employed by a "church," not the kind of work they perform. The plain meaning of "church" includes something greater than the physical building of worship and encompasses the legal entity commonly referred to as a church. The Secretary's definition is too narrow. If Congress wishes to amend the law clearly to change the exemption of church-related school employees, it can do so.

> But, it is not the responsibility or function of the court to perform linguistic gymnastics in order to upset the plain language of Congress as it exists today.[37]

This decision represented the end of the road for the Alabama and Nevada cases since appeal by DOL to the U.S. Supreme Court was held in abeyance (and ultimately never pursued) because of a case pending before that Court involving the same issue: South Dakota's coverage of church-related schools. This case had reached the U.S. Supreme Court on the constitutional grounds that such coverage violated the First and Fourteenth Amendments. When South Dakota, following DOL lead, prepared to tax church-related schools, two of them appealed. The two schools were not separate legal entities. They were part of the churches that ran them. An appeals referee found them subject to tax. The decision was reversed by a County Circuit Court. The South Dakota Supreme Court, by a divided vote, in turn reversed the judgment of the Circuit Court. The case then went to the U.S. Supreme Court.

On May 26, 1981, a unanimous Supreme Court ruled,

> From our reading of the legislation and of its history, we conclude that the only reasonable construction of 26 U.S.C. section 3309(b)(1) is one that exempts petitioners' church-run schools, and others similarly operated, from mandatory state coverage.[38]

The Court argued that Congress drew a distinction between employees "of a church or convention or association of churches" on the one hand and employees of "separately incorporated" organizations on the other. The former would be excluded from coverage under the explicit exclusion of employment for a church, while the latter would be eligible for exclusion under the exclusion relating to employment for an organization operated primarily for religious purposes, but only when the organization is "operated, supervised, controlled, or principally supported by a church or convention or association of churches." The Court found that the individuals performing services for the schools in question were employees of the church and, therefore, exempt. It expressly rejected the DOL interpretation of the term "church" as meaning only the actual house of worship used by a congregation. The Court held instead that "church" refers to the church authorities who conduct the hiring, discharging and directing of church employees.

In a footnote, the Court observed:

> Our holding today concerns only schools that have no legal identity separate from a church. To establish exemption from FUTA, a separately incorporated church school (or other organization) must satisfy the requirements of section 3309(b)(1)(B): (1) that the organization "is operated primarily for religious purposes" and (2) that it is "operated, supervised, controlled, or principally supported by a church or convention or association of churches."

> Because we hold petitioners exempt under section 3309(b)(1)(A), we leave the issue of coverage under section 3309(b)(1)(B) for the future.[39]

Although the Court left open the question of coverage of schools with a legal identity separate from a church, no issues have been presented. This is because unofficial DOL policy has permitted exemption of schools that are "affiliated" with a church, regardless of their separate legal identity. It is not clear what is meant by "affiliated," but in any event, DOL has followed the practice of not objecting to coverage exemptions if the school can demonstrate any affiliation at all with a church, however tenuous or vague the connection.

Experience Rating and Benefit Charging Issues

Before the 1970 Amendments, experience rating issues, often involving questions of how benefits are charged or not charged to employers, constituted the main source of conformity conflicts. The requirement in FUTA for additional tax credit[40] is so broad and ambiguous as to require many interpretations, and these were regularly challenged:

> (1) No reduced rate of contributions . . . is permitted to a person . . . except on the basis of his . . . experience with respect to unemployment or other factors bearing a direct relation to unemployment risk.[41]

The following conformity cases illustrate the various kinds of questions raised under this provision.

Minnesota (1947)

In 1947 Minnesota amended its law to permit employers to make voluntary contributions, in excess of what their tax rates required, for the purpose of building up their reserve accounts and thereby qualifying for tax rate brackets lower than the rates warranted by their actual experience. The contributions could be made subsequent to the close of a rate year, but still affect the rates for that year. The amendment was challenged as running counter to the federal standard on experience rating.

After a conformity hearing on June 10, 1947, the Acting Commissioner of the Social Security Board held that under the federal requirement, any voluntary contributions must be paid no later than the due date for the first quarter contributions in the rate year. This is usually April 30, approximately the 120th day of the new year. Accordingly, the Minnesota provision was ruled out of conformity with the

FUTA. A month later an amendment to the federal law was enacted providing that,

> A State law may, without being deemed to violate the standards set forth in subsection (a), permit voluntary contributions to be used in the computation of reduced rates if such contributions are paid prior to the expiration of 120 days after the beginning of the year for which such rates are effective.[42]

Alabama (1953)

A bill passed by the Alabama legislature in 1953 provided relief from charges for benefits paid their workers who became unemployed because a natural disaster destroyed the employer's business. The Department of Labor took the position that under the bill employers' reduced rates would be determined by a factor—a natural disaster—*other* than their unemployment experience (as measured by benefit charges) and would thus be inconsistent with the federal requirement.

The Administrator of the state agency secured an amendment to the bill providing that the noncharging would not become effective if the Federal Bureau of Employment Security or the Secretary of Labor decided that the bill was not in conformity with federal requirements. The Secretary so decided and the Administrator declared that the bill was not part of the state's unemployment insurance law. The DOL interpretation was changed in 1972 after Pennsylvania and a number of other states sought relief for employers whose businesses were damaged by a severe flood. Under the new interpretation, noncharging is permitted, but only in jurisdictions declared disaster areas by the President pursuant to the Disaster Relief Act.[43]

Michigan (1957)

In 1957 Michigan amended its law covering the cancellation of negative balances. Under the reserve ratio system of experience rating, when all past charges against an employer's account exceed all past contributions credited to the account, his account is considered to have a negative balance. He is usually assigned the highest rates under the state law, which continue until the account balance becomes positive. The accounts of employers who have had only a single year of very heavy unemployment may take a long time to recover. For this reason, many states permit "negative balance employers" the option of having their record wiped clean. If this is permitted, however, the federal experience rating standard (for additional tax credit) was interpreted to require that the employer whose negative balance was cancelled be considered in the position of a new employer. Accordingly, after cancellation, he should serve at least three years before he could qualify for a "reduced rate," a rate below the standard rate of 2.7 percent. Although the federal law was changed in 1954 to permit states to assign new employers reduced rates on the basis of as little as one year's experience, the experience rating requirement was interpreted as requiring three years after cancellation before former negative balance employers could qualify for a rate below 2.7 percent.

The state's Attorney General, in Opinion No. 3109, interpreted the Michigan amendment to mean that employers whose balances were cancelled in 1955, 1956 and 1957 were not required after rate year 1958 to pay the standard 2.7 percent rate or more. In other words, an employer whose negative balance had been cancelled would be permitted a reduced rate before he had three years of experience following the cancellation. This interpretation conflicted with the existing federal policy on the matter and the law was challenged.

The conformity hearing was held October 22, 1957, and was adjourned October 26, 1957 at the request of the state agency. The Michigan law was amended to require a contribution rate of at least 2.7 percent for three years after the last cancellation of negative balances. On October 31, 1957, the Secretary of Labor signed an order dismissing the proceedings.

Oregon (1976)

In 1973 Oregon amended its law to allow a small group of food processors (those who ship 75 percent or more of their annual production in interstate or foreign commerce) to be relieved of some or all charges for benefits paid their workers. The proportion noncharged, determined by a special formula, varied from 10 to 100 percent. All other Oregon employers continued to be charged in accordance with the state's experience rating formula under which benefits paid a worker were charged to his base-period employers in the same proportion to total benefits as the wages paid the worker by the employer were to the worker's total base-period wages. The new noncharging provision took effect on July 1, 1974, and first affected the contribution rates of Oregon employers for the tax year beginning January 1, 1976.

Following enactment of the provision, the Oregon agency requested a finding of conformity by the Secretary of Labor. By letter, dated June 6, 1974, the Secretary advised the agency of his finding that the noncharging provision was inconsistent with the requirements of the experience rating standard in the FUTA. At the agency's request, a hearing was held on June 24, 1976 in Washington.

In a decision issued October 26, 1976, Secretary Usery pointed out that

The test for acceptability of noncharging provisions consistently used by the Department to assure that all employers are charged by the same rule over the same period of time, is one of reasonableness in the measurement of each employer's experience in relation to other employers and to the purposes of experience rating.

He concluded that the Oregon law, in singling out food processors for special treatment, violated "this aforementioned principle of reasonableness." Accordingly, the state law was not in conformity with the federal law.

The main objection to the Oregon provision was basically that employers in a specified group with unfavorable experience could qualify for lower tax rates than employers outside the group with better experience, at least as measured by the factor of benefit charges. That result was the reverse of what was intended by the requirement.

Delaware, New Jersey, New York, Pennsylvania (1979)

FUTA requires states to offer nonprofit organizations and state and local governments the option of financing benefit costs either by paying contributions, as other employers, or permit them to

> . . . elect, for such minimum period and at such time as may be provided by State law, to pay (in lieu of such contributions) into the State unemployment fund amounts equal to the amounts of compensation attributable under the State law to such service.[44]

The provision, part of the 1970 amendments, was interpreted by DOL as prohibiting any noncharging of benefits to employers electing the reimbursement method. The reason was that "as self-insurers, they are fully liable for every dollar of benefits paid their employees and wholly immune from any other costs."[45] DOL pointed out that if a reimbursing employer were relieved of benefit charges, liability for the noncharged benefits would fall to contributing employers in the form of "pooled costs," from which reimbursing employers are exempt. In the aftermath of the 1976 amendments, which added substantially more employing units eligible for the reimbursement option, DOL found it necessary to reiterate its interpretation. The language of the federal provision requires reimbursers to pay amounts "equal" to the benefits based on service with them. Any noncharging, according to DOL, would result in the employer paying an amount *less* than that equal to the benefits. The Department went so far as to insist on full reimbursement even when the benefits were paid erroneously on the basis of an error made by the state agency. Only if overpaid benefits were recovered may the employer be relieved from liability by refunding to him the recovered funds. In many instances, of course, such erroneously paid benefits are not recovered.[46]

Delaware, New Jersey and New York maintained that the language of the statute requiring reimbursing employers to pay for unemployment compensation "attributable under the state law to such service" meant that the state has the right to determine whether or not benefits under particular situations are attributable to service with the employer, or to other factors. DOL rejected this argument, holding that "attributable under the state law" merely meant whether or not the benefits would normally be the employer's responsibility, given the system and order of benefit charging set forth in the state law. A conformity hearing on the issue was held on August 8, 1979 with these states.

A separate hearing was held August 21, 1979 with Pennsylvania on the same issue as well as two other unrelated issues (described earlier in this chapter under *Coverage Issues*). In both cases, the Administrative Law Judges rejected the DOL argument concerning noncharging and concluded, in their recommended decisions, that the Secretary of Labor should find the states' practices (of relieving reimbursing employers of charges under certain circumstances such as erroneous payments) consistent with the federal provision on reimbursement. The Department had argued that benefits paid to ineligible claimants were compensation because all money withdrawn from a state's unemployment fund must be used only for compensation (and certain refunds), pursuant to federal provisions governing the withdrawal of funds. If these are not benefits, then funds are being withdrawn in violation of the withdrawal standards. Pennsylvania's position was that the withdrawal standards were not controlling or even relevant. The question was whether the employer should be charged, not whether money was properly withdrawn from the unemployment fund. The state argued that the FUTA requires that reimbursing employers pay only "amounts of compensation attributable under state law to . . . service" in their employ. The terms "attributable" and "service" are not defined. Benefits paid to ineligible claimants are *not* attributable to service in the employ of any employer, but are attributable to administrative errors by the state agency.

The Administrative Law Judge found that since the FUTA relates compensation to service attributable "under state law" to an employer, state law should be controlling:

> Absent some indication of Congressional intent that the reimbursing employer should be liable for costs incurred through errors, which it does not cause, over which it has no control, and no opportunity to prevent, I cannot accept the Department of Labor's argument.[47]

The only legislative history produced by DOL to support its position was a 1966 Senate Report referring to the reimbursement method as "a form of self-insurance."[48] As

Pennsylvania pointed out, however, the reimbursing employer is far different from that of a true self-insurer. Benefits are not paid directly to the employer but are dispersed from public funds for a public purpose, not to discharge an obligation or liability of a particular employer. Moreover, although Congress intended for employers to weigh the risks in deciding whether to elect the reimbursement option, it did not intend to include risks such as erroneous payments which no employer could prevent, indirectly recover, or estimate.

The Secretary of Labor found on October 31, 1979 that whether compensation paid out is attributable to service with a reimbursing employer is determined by state law. As long as determinations that certain benefits are not attributable under the state law to service with a reimbursing employer are reasonable, such benefits may be noncharged consistently with federal law.[49]

Labor Standards Issues

The labor standards, part of the original Social Security Act, set limits on the states' freedom to establish penalties for refusing a job.[50] They were aimed as much at protecting existing work standards as they were intended to keep claimants from having to accept substandard jobs. They prohibit a state from denying benefits for refusal of new work if the work is vacant due to a labor dispute, if the job interferes with the claimant's freedom to join a union of his choice, or if the wages, hours or working conditions are less favorable than those prevailing for similar work in the locality.

Although most labor standards issues in recent years had concerned the prevailing wage requirement, the conformity confrontations in the early years were over the requirement prohibiting benefit denial for refusing a job vacant due to a labor dispute. Also involved was (and is) the concept of "new work" within the meaning of the labor standards.

Oregon (1938)

The first conformity hearing of the unemployment insurance program involved an issue arising from the labor standards provisions of the Social Security Act. The standards prohibit, as a condition for tax credit, denial of benefits to an otherwise eligible individual for refusing to accept new work "if the position offered is vacant due directly to a strike, lockout or other labor dispute."[51]

In 1938 Oregon voters approved a statutory initiative "regulating picketing and boycotting by labor groups and organizations." Effective December 1, 1938, the approved law defined the term "labor dispute" as follows:

> Whenever in any statute or other law of this state the term 'labor dispute' is used, such term is hereby defined for all purposes to mean and include an actual bona fide controversy in which the disputants stand in proximate relation of employer and the majority of his or its employees and which directly concerns matters directly pertaining to wages, hours, or working conditions of the employees of the particular employer directly involved in such controversy. Disputes between organizations or groups of employees as to which shall act for the employees in dealing with the employer shall not be classed as labor disputes, and the refusal of an employer to deal with either party to any such jurisdictional controversy shall not operate to make the dispute a labor dispute within the meaning of this Act.[52]

By eliminating jurisdictional disputes, the bill resulted in a definition of "labor dispute" that was narrower than the federal law definition. In other words, under the amended state law an individual could be disqualified for refusing a job vacant because of a jurisdictional dispute. A jurisdictional dispute constituted a labor dispute under the federal law. The state law, so amended, was challenged.

After a hearing held December 19, 1938, the Social Security Board found the Oregon law out of conformity. On January 26, 1939, the Oregon legislature rescinded the provision in question, effective back to the date of its enactment. In its decision of January 28, 1939, the Social Security Board found that as of December 31, 1938 the state law included the appropriate federal law labor standards and that the state law was eligible for certification to the Secretary of the Treasury for the taxable year 1938.

California and Washington (1949)

In 1948 West Coast maritime unions were engaged in a labor dispute. In the State of Washington there was also a dispute involving members of a carpenters' union. Some of the workers who were members of the unions engaged in the labor disputes had become unemployed before the disputes for reasons not connected with the disputes, and some were receiving benefits prior to the disputes. All union members, including these workers, were disqualified in California and Washington after the disputes began.

The Federal Bureau of Employment Security advised the two states that the disqualification of those union members unemployed prior to the labor disputes was inconsistent with one of the labor standards provisions of FUTA. That provision prohibits denial of benefits solely on the ground that the worker has refused new work vacant because of the strike, lockout or other labor dispute. The Bureau argued that the struck work was "new work" for those workers unemployed prior to the dispute.

Following a conformity hearing held for both states in December 1949, Secretary of Labor Tobin found that the State of Washington's action violated the federal standard.

Washington brought itself into conformity before the end of the year by changing the interpretation of the law. California agreed to reconsider its decision during the hearing, and the case was dropped. This case provoked the Knowland Amendment (discussed under *Labor Standards* in chapter 2) enacted in 1950, which provides, in part, that no hearing can be called by the Secretary as long as further administrative or judicial review of the matter is available to the parties under the state law.

California (1955)

This case involved California's reconsideration of the same issue that precipitated the 1949 hearing. The California Supreme Court in 1955 affirmed the reimposed disqualification of the claimants under the labor dispute disqualification provision on the grounds that all of the work for seamen on the waterfront was "their work," not "new work," because of their union's agreements with the employer association.

Following a formal hearing, the federal hearing officer appointed by the Secretary of Labor observed that all members of the unions registered at the hiring halls had a *group* attachment to and shared equally in all available work for seamen on the waterfront and that when a work stoppage occurred, all registered workers had left "their work" because of the labor dispute. However, claimants were free to negotiate individually for continued employment with the same employer. It could be argued, therefore, that their prior contract had terminated and their old jobs were now "new work." In any event, upon the advice of an informal panel of legal authorities, appointed by the Secretary to review the findings of the hearing officer, the Secretary found that the state had not violated the federal standard.[53]

Fair Hearing and Promptness Issues

On April 26, 1971, a unanimous Supreme Court decided one of the most important UI cases to reach the courts. It involved interpretation of the phrase "when due" in the Social Security Act provision requiring states to provide such methods of administration as are found by the Secretary of Labor to be reasonably calculated to insure full payment of benefits "when due."[54] The Court concluded that the word "due" means "the time when payments are first administratively allowed as a result of a hearing of which both parties have notice and are permitted to present their respective positions. . . ."[55] This decision resulted in amendments to every state UI law and dramatic changes in the promptness and quality of UI appeals proceedings and in the promptness of benefit payments to eligible claimants.

The Java Case (1971)

Unlike all other issues discussed in this chapter, the *Java* case was not a federal-state confrontation, although it was later the cause of considerable intergovernmental conflict and cooperation. It has not been uncommon for UI issues to be raised by individuals or groups of claimants or employers, with the states and DOL being the common adversary. Usually these are state court cases and a federal-state conflict arises when a state court interprets a state UI law provision in such a way as to violate federal requirements. In recent years more UI cases (e.g., County of Los Angeles) have appeared in federal courts. The *Java* case has been one of the most important.

The case involved two California claimants, Carroll H. Hudson and Judith Java, who were awarded benefits following an eligibility interview at which the employer did not appear. Payments began immediately. The employer, who is given ten days to appeal, challenged eligibility in each case.

Pursuant to the California law, payments were automatically stopped pending decision on the employer's appeal. The median delay in resuming payments after an employer filed an appeal, assuming that the claimant's eligibility is upheld, was about seven weeks. The claimants appealed the state's stoppage of payments to the U.S. District Court for the Northern District of California.[56] The claimants argued first that the intent of the state UI program, to stave off extreme personal hardship as well as society-wide depression in terms of increasing unemployment, is clearly thwarted when a claimant must wait some 50 days for payments to resume. Second, they argued that the state law violates the provision of the Social Security Act which requires state laws to provide methods of administration "reasonably calculated to insure full payment of unemployment compensation when due." Third, they argued that the denial of benefits, without a prior hearing, to persons already found eligible violates their rights to due process of law under the Constitution. They cited a March 23, 1970 decision of the U.S. Supreme Court in *Goldberg* v. *Kelley,* 397 U.S. 254 (1970), that a welfare claimant's benefits not be terminated without first affording him an opportunity for a full evidentiary hearing. Consistent with that case, they argued that once UI benefits are allowed, they should continue until there is a hearing on the employer's appeal and a decision favorable to the employer.

California argued that a decision in favor of the plaintiffs would adversely affect the UI program in California and 46 other states. "A substantial alteration in processing claims of such magnitude would have a serious financial impact on the State of California and impose on it a crushing administrative burden." More important, the state argued that the agency's administrative determination that a claimant is entitled to benefits is not sufficient, standing alone, to justify payment until a determination is made on the employer's appeal. Prior to hearing on the employer's appeal, no testimony is taken under oath: there is no right to confrontation or to call witnesses. Moreover, since employers were successful in 47 percent of their appeals, benefits paid out which were subsequently held to be valid would have amounted to $800,000 if the state had been required to pay benefits during the pendency of any employer appeal. These benefits would have been unrecoverable because of the state law provision requiring waiver of recoupment if benefits had been received without fault on the part of the recipient. Furthermore, recovery would be against equity and good conscience.

The state argued that its procedure balances administrative prudence and claimants' rights, whereas if benefits were payable pending an employer's appeal, the balance would be altered because claimants would then have incentive to delay hearings and decisions, thereby adding to the administrative burden and financial loss to the state. The state rejected the applicability of *Goldberg* v. *Kelley*. In that case, it was important that termination of welfare payments be undertaken only after a full evidentiary hearing, since withholding of these payments rendered those receiving welfare literally destitute. The state argued that UI claimants were in a different position from welfare recipients:

> Plaintiffs (UI claimants) here have admittedly suffered considerable inconvenience but they are, however, receiving welfare benefits. True these benefits are modest, but plaintiffs are only asked to maintain themselves on such a modest scale for approximately 30 to 45 days, during which a decision on the appeal is being made.[57]

In other words, the UI claimants were not as destitute as the plaintiffs in *Goldberg* since they would receive welfare, as in fact they did at the time.

In its brief,[58] DOL argued in support of the California practice in that it was more reasonable than the alternative, urged by the plaintiffs, of paying benefits pursuant to an initial determination and until reversed by an appeals body. According to the brief, that procedure would create substantial overpayments, as seen retroactively, cause delay in hearings, and result in more close issues being decided initially against claimants to avoid overpayments. DOL argued that if the decision in *Goldberg* v. *Kelley* applied to UI (no termination except after a full hearing) the practical effect would be for states to deny benefits to every claimant until after a hearing and a decision by a referee that the claimant was eligible. DOL also pointed out that unlike welfare recipients, UI claimants are not usually destitute. Finally, the DOL brief argued that the California procedure (as well as that in 46 other states) was consistent with the federal requirement of "payment of unemployment compensation when due." The original draft bills prepared by the Social Security Board to help states design their first UI laws so as to meet conformity requirements, contained suggested legislative language providing for withholding benefits pending an appeal. These provisions were in the Alabama law when the Supreme Court upheld its constitutionality in 1936. They also provided the model for the California provision.

In a short, eight page decision, the U.S. District Court ruled the California provision defective on both constitutional and statutory grounds:[59]

> By not providing a pre-termination hearing, it runs counter to the principles enunciated in *Goldberg* v. *Kelley, cit. supra.* And by being applied so as to result in a median seven week delay in payments to claimants who have been found eligible for such payments, the California statute violates the directive of 42 U.S.C. 503(a)(1).

The Court found the present case "indistinguishable" from *Goldberg*.

As here, the defendants in *Goldberg* argued the State's interest in protecting public funds. The Supreme Court, balancing this interest against the welfare recipient in having the necessities of life while the bureaucracy mulls over his continued eligibility, found the fiscal argument somewhat weak, and rejected it. Defendants herein suggest that the unemployed person is perhaps not in such dire straits as the recipient of public assistance, in that he can always go on welfare, and thus save himself from absolute destitution. It is scant comfort to the disaster stricken that there is someone, somewhere, worse off than he, and this Court finds that the situation of the unemployed person herein is every bit as lamentable as that of the welfare client. . . .

The most fundamental purpose of both the federal and the state unemployment compensation laws is 'to *prevent* the burden of injured employees becoming charges upon society.'[60]

On April 26, 1971, Chief Justice Burger delivered, for a unanimous Supreme Court, an opinion holding that the California provision violated Section 303(a)(1) of the Social Security Act.[61] That made it unnecessary to rule on the constitutional issue involved in *Goldberg* on which the District Court relied. Specifically, it violated the requirement of that section that the state law provide such methods of administration "as are found by the Secretary of Labor to be reasonably calculated to insure full payment of unemployment compensation when due."

Reviewing the history of the Social Security Act led the Court to:

. . . the conclusion that 'when due' was intended to mean at the earliest stage of unemployment that such payments were administratively feasible after giving both the worker and the employer an opportunity to be heard.

According to the Court,

> Probably no program could be devised to make insurance payments available precisely on the nearest payday following the termination, but to the extent that this was administratively feasible this must be regarded as what Congress was trying to accomplish.
>
> . . . . . .
>
> We conclude that the word 'due' in section 303(a)(1), when construed in light of the purposes of the Act, means the time when payments are first administratively allowed as a result of a hearing of which both parties have notice and are permitted to present their respective positions; any other construction would fail to meet the objective of early substitute compensation during unemployment.
>
> . . . . . .
>
> Our reading of the statute imposes no hardship on either the State or the employer and gives effect to the congressional objective of getting money into the pocket of the unemployed worker at the earliest point that is administratively feasible. That is what the Unemployment Insurance Program was all about.

The Court found the California local office's initial interview an adequate pre-determination fact-finding proceeding in which the claims of both the employer and the employee can be heard.

Although the eligibility interview is informal and does not contemplate taking evidence in the traditional judicial sense, it has adversary characteristics and the minimum obligation of an employer is to inform the interviewer and the claimant of any disqualifying factors. So informed, the interviewer can direct the initial inquiry to identifying a frivolous or dilatory contention by either party.

Aftermath of Java

On June 14, 1971, DOL advised all state agencies of the implications of *Java*. [62] First, if benefits have been awarded a claimant pursuant to an initial determination, they may not be suspended pending an appeal period or pending, as in California, disposition of an employer's appeal. That meant changes in 47 states' laws or interpretations. Second, states must provide reasonable notice to both the claimant and employer of the time and place of the pre-determination fact-finding hearing. This new step required changes, not in state laws, but in virtually every state's procedures, since no state at that time provided such notices. Finally,

To keep to a minimum the impact of overpayments that may result from modifications or reversals of benefit determinations on appeals, attention needs to be given not only to quality at the determination level but also to expediting the processing of all appeals.

The reduction of overpayments was one reason to focus on appeals promptness. The estimated magnitude of overpayments, nationally, had the *Java* requirements been operative in fiscal year 1971, would have been about $7.5 million. There were other reasons. During 1971, the states decided fewer than one-fourth of their benefit appeals within 30 days and less than half within 45 days. In some states, practically no appeals were processed within 30 days and relatively few within 45 days. Over one-fourth of all appellants waited more than 75 days for a decision.

In 1971, over a dozen suits were filed in federal courts which either directly or collaterally sought relief from the delays of the benefit appeals process. In December 1971, a Federal District Court concluded that even Vermont's average five to six week delay (then among the shortest in the nation) was unreasonable. On April 14, 1972, a complaint was filed in a Federal District Court charging that Georgia's failure to conduct hearings promptly (it averaged 3 percent of decisions issues within 30 days) was violative of the Fourteenth Amendment and Section 303(a)(1) of the Social Security Act.

In 1973 Connecticut's informal determination procedure was challenged. A U.S. District Court had enjoined the Connecticut agency from denying claimants benefits under its existing eligibility determination procedure without first providing a constitutionally sufficient hearing. The District Court was persuaded of the need for a full hearing at the initial determination level because Connecticut's record in hearing appeals was the slowest in the nation. The state appealed this ruling. In a decision issued January 14, 1975,[63] the U.S. Supreme Court made it clear that unless appeals decisions are issued promptly, states would face the costly prospect of making the initial determination process more like a full "due process" hearing. The Supreme Court held,

> In this context, the possible length of wrongful deprivation of unemployment benefits is an important factor in assessing the impact of official action on the private interests. . . . Prompt and adequate administrative review provides an opportunity for correction of errors made in initial eligibility determinations. Thus the rapidity of administrative

review is a significant factor in assessing the suffi-
ciency of the entire process.

The Supreme Court vacated the District Court's judgment
and remanded the case for reconsideration in light of the fact
that while the case was pending, Connecticut completely
revised its appeals structure in order to accelerate the process.

DOL advised the states:

> The Court's decision makes crucial the need for all
> States to meet and maintain at least the levels of ap-
> peals performance prescribed in the Secretary's Ap-
> peals Promptness Standard.[64]

The Appeals Performance Standard, described in the section
on *Administration* in chapter 2, was the product of *Java* and
specifically a commitment by DOL in its brief to the Court:

> The Secretary of Labor is cognizant of the need for
> increased promptness and, insofar as it is possible
> to shorten the delay without denying a fair hearing
> to the participants, he intends to effectuate im-
> provements. (Footnote: The Secretary is presently
> considering the wisdom and feasibility of pro-
> mulgating a specific federal standard of the time
> within which each State must complete its pro-
> cedures for determining whether benefits are
> due.)[65]

An Appeals Promptness Project, generated by the penden-
cy of *Java* and organized to implement the Secretary's commitment, issued a comprehensive report July 1972. It identified a number of contributing factors to the states' poor
promptness record, including inadequate staffing, ineffective management, outmoded processing systems and inflexi-
ble budgeting. The root cause was simply stated:

> The basic problem is the failure at State and na-
> tional levels to insist on promptness and on doing
> those things which would produce promptness.[66]

The Report included a number of recommendations, including a performance standard.

Java's influence was not limited to the appeals area.
DOL's failure to insist on promptness was not confined to
states' appeals performance. It had similarly failed to require
a reasonable degree of promptness in paying benefits. First
payment time lapse (the speed with which a state agency
makes its first payment of benefits) performance was was
abysmal as appeals time lapse. DOL had established suggested criteria for reasonable time lapse calling for 86 percent of intrastate claims to be paid within 14 days beginning
with the week ending date of the first compensable week,
and 67 percent of interstate claims. From 1971 through 1975
there were never more than 22 states that met the intrastate
criterion in any given calendar quarter, and never more than
15 states met the interstate criterion.

As happened in the appeals area, by 1975, poor performance of promptness of first payments resulted in court
cases in Florida, Georgia, Illinois, Kentucky, Maryland and
Virginia. A Federal District Court in Illinois, appalled by the
long time lapse of that state, concluded that the state agency
did not adhere to the requirements of Section 303(a)(1) of the
Social Security Act. Although it did not determine that DOL
had improperly certified the state for granted funds, it did
determine that the state was not making payments "when
due." The Court concluded that the "when due" requirement meant that the state agency must mail checks out
within 14 days from the end of the first compensable week of
unemployment in all cases in which the claimant has provided all necessary information, and external factors beyond the
agency's control do not intervene. The agency must mail

checks for all subsequent valid claims within 14 days from the end of the last compensable week of each bi-weekly claim period.[67]

It became obvious that unless DOL developed a promptness standard (rather than merely guidelines) the courts would do so. And different courts may well develop different standards. On March 5, 1976, a proposed Standard for Benefit Payment Promptness was published in the Federal Register:

> . . . responsive to the overriding concern of the United States Supreme Court in . . . *Java* . . .and that of other courts with delays in the payment of unemployment compensation to eligibile individuals.[68]

The proposed Standard was adopted July 23, 1976. It was later revised to be less stringent, effective August 28, 1978.

NOTES

1. Sections 3304(a)(1), FUTA and 303(a)(2), SSA.

2. Section 303(a)(8), SSA permits a state to receive administrative grants only if expended solely for purposes and in the amounts found necessary by the Secretary of Labor for the proper and efficient administration of the state law.

3. Sections 3304(a)(4), FUTA and 303(a)(5), SSA.

4. Section 303(a)(1),SSA.

5. Section 3304(a)(6), FUTA.

6. Section 3304(c), FUTA.

7. Section 3306(c), FUTA.

8. Section 3309, FUTA.

9. Section 3304(a)(6)(A), FUTA.

10. Decision of Secretary of Labor John T. Dunlop, June 6, 1975, in the *Matter of the Question of Whether the State of New York's Unemployment Insurance Law Conforms with the Requirements of the Federal Unemployment Tax Act.*

11. *Ibid.*

12. *Ibid.*

13. Section 3304(a)(6)(A), FUTA.

14. Pennsylvania Unemployment Compensation Law, section 402.1(2).

15. Section 3304(a)(6)(A), FUTA.

16. Public Law 95-171, approved November 12, 1977.

17. Message accompanying Veto of H.B. 47, June 23, 1978.

18. Under New Hampshire's law all claimants' benefit years begin and end the same date (April 1 through March 31). All base periods are the preceding calendar year. In all other states these periods vary for each individual depending on when he first files for benefits.

19. Section 3304(c), FUTA.

20. 616 F.2d 240.

21. Preamble to H.B. 808.

22. *National League of Cities* v. *Usery,* 426 U.S. 833 (1976).

23. Charles C. Mulcahy (Mulcahy and Wherry) to Bernard F. Hillenbrand, Executive Director, National Association of Counties, and Ralph Tubor, Director, Federal Affairs, National Association of Counties, Summary of Legal Opinion on the Constitutionality of the Unemployment Compensation Amendments of 1976, March 16, 1977.

24. Charles S. Rhyne (Rhyne and Rhyne) to all Plaintiffs Participating in the Constitutional Challenge to the Federal Unemployment Compensation Program, P.L. No. 94-566 (H.R. 10210).

25. Memorandum Opinion of United States District Judge Charles R. Richey, United States District Court for the District of Columbia, C.A. No. 77-2023, December 29, 1977.

26. *Ibid.*

27. *Steward Machine Co.* v. *Davis,* 301 U.S. 548 (1937).

28. Opinion of United States Court of Appeals for the District of Columbia Circuit No. 77-2138, *The County of Los Angeles, California, et al.* v. *Marshall;* No. 78-1142, *The County of Los Angeles, California, Louisiana Municipal Association, et al.* v. *Marshall,* March 19, 1980.

29. 616 F.2d 240.

30. Section 3309, FUTA.

31. *Trinity Evangelical Lutheran Church* v. *Department of Industrial Relations,* No. CV 78 500 325 Cir. Court, Mobile County, Alabama (January 27, 1979).

32. *Ibid.* Also, *Roman Catholic Church* v. *State of Louisiana,* No. 219,660, 19th Jud. Dist. Ct., East Baton Rouge Parish, LA (August 31, 1979). *Grace Brethren* v. *State of California,* Case No. CV 79-93, USDC CD California (September 21, 1979).

33. Title II of the Emergency Jobs and Unemployment Assistance Act of 1974—Public Law 93-567, approved December 31, 1974.

34. *Unemployment Compensation Amendments of 1975,* Report No. 94-755, Committee on Ways and Means, House of Representatives, 94th Cong., 1st Sess. (December 16, 1975), p. 17.

35. *Unemployment Compensation Amendments of 1976,* Report No. 94-1265, Committee on Finance, U.S. Senate, 94th Cong., 2nd Sess. (September 20, 1976), p. 8.

36. *State of Alabama* v. *Marshall* - No. 79-3968, *State of Nevada* v. *Marshall* - No. 79-4032, in the United States Court of Appeals for the Fifth District, September 8, 1980.

37. *Ibid.*

38. *St. Martin Evangelical Lutheran Church and Northwestern Lutheran Academy* v. *State of South Dakota,* No. 80-120, May 26, 1981.

39. *Ibid.*

40. See discussion of tax offset approach in *Providing an Incentive* in chapter 1 for distinction between additional and normal tax credit.

41. Section 3303(a)(1), FUTA.

42. Section 3303(d), FUTA.

43. U.S. Department of Labor, Unemployment Insurance Program Letter No. 1211, November 14, 1972.

44. Section 3309(a)(2), FUTA.

45. U.S. Department of Labor, Manpower Administration, *Draft Legislation to Implement the Employment Security Amendments of 1970—H.R. 14705* (1970), p. 104.

46. U.S. Department of Labor, Employment and Training Administration, *Draft Language and Commentary to Implement the Unemploy-*

ment Compensation Amendments of 1976—P.L. 94-566 (Supplement #4, Questions and Answers, September 1, 1977), p. 16.

47. Recommended Decision rendered by Administrative Law Judge Briggs, October 11, 1979, and served on all parties on October 12, 1979.

48. Report No. 1425, Senate 1966, p. 10.

49. *Conformity Proceedings ETA-1 (1979), Federal Register,* Vol. 44, No. 216, November 6, 1979, p. 64369.

50. Section 3304(a)(5), FUTA.

51. *Ibid.*

52 Oregon Employment Division Law.

53. William Haber and Merrill G. Murray, *Unemployment Insurance in the American Economy* (Homewood, IL: Richard D. Irwin, Inc., 1966), p. 448.

54. Section 303(a)(1), SSA.

55. *Java* v. *California Department of Human Resources Development,* 402 U.S. 1 21 (1971).

56. *Java* v. *California Department of Human Resources Development,* Case No. C-69-350 ACW, USDC ND California (December 5, 1969).

57. *Ibid.*

58. *Ibid.*

59. *Ibid.*

60. *Ibid.* The U.S. District Court quoted from Chief Justice Gibson in *Abelleira, et al.* v. *The District Court of Appeals, etc.,* 17 C.2d 280, 300, 1941; California Unemployment Insurance Code.

61. *Java* v. *California Department of Human Resources Development,* 402 U.S. 1 21 (1971).

62. U.S. Department of Labor, Unemployment Insurance Program Letter No. 1126, June 14, 1971.

63. *Fusari, Commissioner of Labor* v. *Steinberg, et al.,* appeal from the U.S. District Court for the District of Connecticut, No. 73-848, January 14, 1975.

64. U.S. Department of Labor, Unemployment Insurance Program Letter No. 8-75 (1975).

65. Quoted in U.S. Department of Labor, *Promptness in Unemployment Benefit Appeals Decisions—A Report and Recommendations,* July 1972, p. 19.

66. *Ibid.,* p. 2.

67. *Sylvester Burtton, et al.* v. *Holland, et al.;* USDC ND I11 - ED, No. 75 Civ. 892.

68. *Standard for Benefit Payment Promptness, Federal Register,* Vol. 41, No. 45, March 5, 1976, para. 610.1.

Chapter 6
Summary, Trends, Conclusions

The Conceptual and Legislative Framework

As envisioned by President Roosevelt's Committee on Economic Security, unemployment insurance, like the American system of federalism, was to operate as a hybrid, with federal and state governments each having principal jurisdiction over particular aspects of the program and both sharing responsibility for others. As described in chapter 1, the immediate federal role—to inspire states to enact UI programs—was to be accomplished through a federal payroll tax and a provision allowing employers credit against most of that tax for the taxes they paid under a state UI program that met federal requirements.

A second federal responsibility involved management of the funds collected under the program. All taxes collected, state and federal, were required to be deposited in the National Treasury. State deposits remained state property, but any money withdrawn could be used only for the purpose of paying unemployment compensation.

The third major federal responsibility was to establish national standards in areas where uniformity was absolutely essential. The two devices or sanctions available for insuring state conformity were denial of employers' credit against the federal tax and withholding of federal grants for administration.

The states were to be responsible for enacting complete, self-contained unemployment insurance laws that conformed to federal standards. The states would have almost complete freedom to establish qualifying conditions for benefits, weekly amount and duration of benefits, eligibility and disqualification conditions, and employer tax systems. Administrative responsibilities were to be shared by both levels of government. Primary responsibility for administering their laws fell to the states, but the federal partner would have control over allocation of all funds for administrative expenses, authority to insure that administrative grants were used by the states only for proper purposes, and an obligation to provide technical assistance to the states.

As described in chapter 2, with a few exceptions, the 1935 Social Security Act embodied the recommendations of the Committee on Economic Security. Through the federal unemployment tax and tax credit device, the unemployment insurance titles of the Act provided the impetus for quick enactment of UI laws in every state. They established the basic division of responsibilities between federal and state governments. Federal powers were spelled out explicitly, and as with the U.S. Constitution, those powers not expressly delegated to the federal partner or those that could not reasonably be implied as federal, were reserved to the states. Unlike the Constitution, the Social Security Act could be amended or abolished by Congress alone. Unemployment insurance would be a federal-state system only as long as that arrangement appeared to Congress to provide advantages.

Experience

Checks and Balances

A legislative framework under which authority and responsibilities for a program are divided between two partners will soon collapse unless there are means to restrain either partner from encroaching on the authority of the other. The U.S. Constitution provides for an elaborate system of checks and balances among the three branches of the federal government as well as between the federal and state governments. The Social Security Act provides some checks and balances. The American political system provides others. Among them are the following:

- State authority to enact provisions contrary to federal requirements is checked by the consequences of denial of tax credit and loss of administrative grants;
- Federal authority to substitute a federal system for the federal-state system is checked by a state-oriented Congress;
- State authority to enact conforming but extreme provisions is checked by federal power to enact uniform standards;
- Federal authority to radically alter the system is offset by public acceptance of the basic provisions of unemployment insurance;
- State authority over the administration of its program is checked by federal control of administrative grants;
- Federal authority to impose sanctions on nonconforming states is checked by Congressional aversion to penalizing a state.

There are more. Until recent years, the result of these checks has been to restrain the actions of each partner so as to achieve something of a balance of power, with neither dominating in the control of the unemployment insurance system.

Conflicts

Since the beginning, the program has been characterized by two types of conflicts—those caused by particular provisions of law and others generated by friction between two levels of government having responsibilities for a single program. Conflict over specific provisions is carried on almost every year within the 53 jurisdictions with UI laws between individuals and organizations with different views of the purposes of unemployment insurance. When debate between business and labor has been relatively even, the result has usually been beneficial to the program. Open fights over substantive program provisions are the source of the program's vitality. More than any other single factor, this controversy has kept state programs flexible and responsive to local needs and attitudes.

The second type of conflict, intergovernmental, is inevitable in a program where responsibilities are divided, and federal and state governments have different perspectives. For example, state authorities with day-to-day responsibility for administration of their programs are bound to collide with federal officials who control the amount of money available for administration, set the priorities for the money, and may even dictate the "methods" the state must apply in carrying out administrative functions. These kinds of conflicts have not had a particularly beneficial impact on the program, but neither have they been harmful.

State and federal differences over the meaning of the federal law are more significant intergovernmental conflicts. As described in chapter 4, most have been settled through a variety of approaches. When negotiation has failed, the system provides a mechanism, the conformity process, whereby the issue may be resolved. It insures a state a fair hearing, a full opportunity to present its views and the option to seek judicial review of an adverse decision. As discussed in chapter 5, the most difficult and significant UI issues have been settled in this fashion. Interpretations are one means by which federal authority has been expanded to meet particular issues, and the conformity and judicial processes have been testing grounds for the soundness of federal interpretations. The process has been used sparingly, basically because it involves much effort on the part of all parties to present and prepare support for positions. The availability of a fair hearing, if negotiation fails and one is needed, has had the same beneficial effect on the system as the fair hearing opportunity available to claimants and employers.

Cooperation

Conflicts notwithstanding, the dominant pattern of intergovernmental relations has been cooperative effort. This too has been the result of the division of responsibilities and the development of checks on authority. With each level of government restrained by statutory or practical obstacles, it quickly became clear that the program could operate only through cooperation. The interdependence of the two partners was demonstrated at the outset.

As issues arose after the program was inaugurated in most states, interpretations were made of federal law, many with administrative implications. To be realistic and workable, it was necessary that interpretations and decisions affecting administration be developed on the basis of state experience and capability. This required participation of state officials or, at the minimum, opportunity for state review and reaction to proposed decisions and standards. This is an example of state participation in a predominantly federal function. Federal participation in essentially state matters has been discussed in the context of federal recommendations for amendments to state programs. These recommendations were particularly influential at the beginning of the program, as discussed in chapter 1. Over the years the recommendations diminished for the variety of reasons discussed in chapter 4.

Intergovernmental cooperation occurs at all administrative levels and in all aspects of the program. It is the key, for example, to successful negotiation of conformity issues, as described in chapter 4.

Conflicts over the desirability of particular program provisions, discord over the operation of the program, disagreements over the meaning of federal law, and overriding cooperative effort are the ingredients of federal-state relationships that have contributed to the success of unemployment insurance. The two sources of these characteristics are the federal-state division of responsibilities originally spelled out in the Social Security Act, and the legislative, practical, and voluntary checks against arbitrary expansion of authority by either partner. These are the elements that make possible debate in a state capitol over the level of the maximum weekly benefit amount; a U.S. Supreme Court decision upholding the constitutionality of a requirement that states cover state and local government workers as a condition for tax credit; a conformity hearing rejecting a state-imposed income test as a condition for benefits; resolution on an informal basis of a conflict with federal law caused by a state court decision; consideration by a state advisory council of recommendations prepared by the federal government for changes in the state's qualifying requirement.

Attitudes

The unemployment insurance program is significantly affected by the attitudes of those who operate it and, indirectly, by public attitudes—about unemployed workers, claimants, employers, and unemployment insurance.

The system is a product of the 1930s depression when few Americans were without direct or close experience with unemployment. That experience showed that anyone could lose a job through no fault of his own and could remain unemployed despite all reasonable efforts to find work.

Enactment of the UI provisions of the Social Security Act reflected general recognition of government's obligation to provide some degree of protection against a hazard faced by everyone who works for another. These concepts represented radical departures from prevailing attitudes of preceding periods, that equated unemployment with shiftlessness, laziness or other weaknesses of character, and which rejected government support as gratuitous handouts likely only to encourage more idleness.

In the 1930s a number of idealistic individuals were attracted to the new social insurance program at both the federal and state levels. Many developed strong personal commitments to relieving the hardship of unemployment. The system was thus built on the premise that most unemployed workers would rather work than draw benefits and was staffed in significant part by individuals dedicated to making unemployment insurance an effective means of meeting unemployed workers' needs.

The federal leadership established two overall objectives: adequacy and fairness. Recommendations of the Department of Labor and its predecessors constantly stressed the need for adequate benefit amounts and duration, as described in chapter 3. Three Democratic and one Republican administrations supported federal benefit standards to ensure adequacy. States were regularly encouraged to assure that the great majority would be compensated for at least half their weekly wage loss if unemployed, and to establish the maximum weekly benefit amount as a percentage (preferably 66-2/3 percent) of the statewide average weekly wage so that benefit levels would automatically keep pace with increases in wage levels. It was also recommended that the benefit duration allowed either be the same for all claimants (preferably 26 weeks), or be expressed as a maximum amount equal to a substantial fraction (preferably at least 3/5 or 2/3 instead of the common 1/3 fraction) of the claimant's base-period wages, up to no less than 26 times the claimant's weekly benefit amount.

Fairness was stressed as much as adequacy. For example, although the amount of prior employment was the intended measure of labor force attachment, qualifying requirements in some states were expressed in terms of flat dollar amounts of base-period earnings. These tests were discouraged by federal policy recommendations because higher paid workers could meet them with less employment than others. Similarly, states with disqualifications requiring that the claimant must be reemployed and earn a specified flat minimum amount before he can again become eligible for benefits were urged by the Department of Labor to require instead that the minimum amount of new earnings be stated as some specific multiple of the claimant's weekly benefit amount. Low wage workers would thus not be disadvantaged in meeting the disqualification. States with dependents' allowance provisions were urged not to require more of female claimants in qualifying for such allowances. Special disqualifications for particular categories of workers—students, retirees, pregnant women were discouraged.

Beginning with the first Draft Bill developed by the Social Security Board in 1936, federal efforts to influence state legislation represented for a time the only leadership with regard to program policy issues. They provided focal points for discussion even in states with perspectives wholly different from the federal view. Federally organized legislative planning conferences, where recommendations were debated, brought federal and state officials together. The recommendations, somewhat predictable over time in their emphasis, also provided a certain stability to the program.

In time, as the states gained experience and confidence, many moved more independently concerning policy matters. Moreover, certain interest groups—chiefly employers and labor—acquired greater knowledge about UI and more skills in advancing their positions. The state side of the intergovernmental relationship grew generally stronger as a result; a more equal federal-state balance evolved. While some on each side saw the other partner as too overbearing or too stubbornly independent, for the most part a reasonable climate developed that was favorable to a cooperative and creative relationship.

Recent Trends

Recent years have been marked by increasing federal dominance of the unemployment insurance system. The balance of power has been undermined by new federal standards, program objectives have shifted, and federal-state relations have undergone substantial change. Chapter 3 described federal program standards enacted in these years. The 1980 and 1981 amendments which limit the conditions under which extended benefits may be paid remove from state jurisdiction almost all control over this aspect of unemployment insurance.

These and other recent restrictive program standards have been pressed primarily on the grounds of cost savings. This objective has become compelling rationale, given recent Congressional preoccupation with reducing the federal budget. In addition, cost-saving motivated standards have not been unwelcome in some states which are interested in avoiding tax increases otherwise necessary to keep benefits in step with inflation, to replenish their funds from the drains of recent recessions and to pay back moneys borrowed from the federal loan fund.[1]

These trends toward increasing federal dominance and departure from long-standing program goals are products of dramatic economic and political developments in recent years.

A major indirect contributor to the cost cutting trend was the inclusion of both federal and state UI tax receipts and UI expenditures in the federal unified budget. From 1936 through 1967, state UI tax moneys were not included in the federal administrative budget, which was the basis for determining the size of the federal surplus or deficit. They were not included because they were reserved in trust funds earmarked for employment security purposes and not available for other activities. However, by 1967, total receipts of all U.S. Treasury trust funds (including Social Security's) equaled almost 40 percent of the total administrative budget from which they were excluded. Because of their size and impact on the economy, the UI and other trust funds, both their receipts and expenditures, were incorporated in a unified federal budget beginning in 1968.[2]

The National Commission on Unemployment Compensation unanimously recommended removal of UI trust fund moneys from the federal budget. The Commission argued that the major portion of employer UI taxes is state moneys, not federal. State decisions affecting program matters are more important than federal decisions in their influence on UI revenues and expenditures. The basic reason for the Commission's recommendation, however, was that, as part of the unified federal budget, trust funds have increasingly become the target of intensive efforts by both the executive and legislative branches to cut the expenditure side of the federal budget, frequently without much or any regard to the damage caused by the cuts in the programs involved.[3]

A second source of current cost consciousness is the sudden and deep plunge of several states from solvency into debtor status. Until the 1970s, with few exceptions, states' reserves were generally adequate to cope with the regular fluctuations of the economy. During the severe recession of the mid-1970s, 25 states found it necessary to borrow from the federal loan fund. By 1977 and 1978, unemployment had declined, but the recovery was neither robust nor long enough to enable many states to reestablish adequate reserves. Thirteen states were still in debt at the end of 1979, by which time unemployment was again on the rise. It reached record post-Depression levels in 1982. By the end of that year, 23 states owed the loan fund $10.6 billion. The federal UI trust fund account for extended benefits was also in debt to the Treasury for about $7 billion, most of it for outstanding costs of the Federal Supplemental Benefits program of the mid-1970s.[4]

These economic shocks had enormous impact not only on state reserves, but on the direction the entire unemployment insurance system would take in the foreseeable future. With state as well as federal UI deficits reflected in the federal budget, state programs became subject to budget cutting efforts by Congress and the Administration. The 1980 and 1981 EB amendments described in chapter 3 are examples. The insolvency and potential insolvency of so many states influence the direction of the program also in another way. For these states, the primary consideration has become, first, how to keep the debt from growing, and later, how to repay the debt and rebuild the fund. The federal loan repayment requirements and the recently added requirement of interest to be paid on loans made after March 1982 have had significant influence on state decisions. In addition to the interest, employers in a state that has not repaid its loan within about two years face an annual reduction in their federal tax offset credit until the debt is repaid. This translates into a uniform, progressive 0.3 percent increase in the federal unemployment tax rate each year the debt is outstanding. States have the option of paying an amount equivalent to the FUTA "repayment tax" instead of the amount being collected through the uniform tax rate increases. Thus, states may choose to raise the amount needed through experience-rated taxes, or from any other source.

In some states, regaining a sound financial footing may be accomplished by appropriate increases in the state UI tax rate, tax base, or both. In others it will require, in addition, changes in benefit provisions aimed at reducing expenditures.[5] In any event, being preoccupied with regaining solvency means, in most cases, a moratorium on any liberalization of the benefit formula (even in states where benefit levels are inadequate), and a favorable reception to a wide range of cost cutting measures, from frozen maximum benefit amounts to stiffer disqualifications.

A third source of trends in the early 1980s is, of course, the election in 1980 of a President and Congress committed to reducing the cost of domestic programs generally, and the cost of so-called entitlement programs particularly. The impetus has been both a serious federal deficit as well as a predisposition by many Administration leaders to distrust the motives of those drawing unemployment insurance and other "entitlements."

Testimony on behalf of new restrictive standards reveals an Administration attitude toward the program and unemployed workers quite different from that previously expressed concerning adequacy and fairness. In 1981, for example, U.S. Secretary of Labor Raymond J. Donovan testified on behalf of one of a number of UI amendments proposed by the Reagan Administration. The proposal would require all states to disqualify claimants who, after three months of unemployment, refuse any job within their capabilities paying gross wages equal to the higher of the minimum wage or their weekly benefit amount. The proposal, which was rejected, was similar to that enacted in 1980 to apply to extended benefit claimants.[6] According to the Secretary, the proposal was needed because,

> By allowing unemployed workers to draw up to six
> months of compensation unless jobs in their oc-

cupations are available, the present unemployment compensation system discourages workers from seeking employment in new industries. . . .[7]

A second Administration proposal (enacted) for elimination of the national trigger for extended benefits was described by a DOL spokesman as necessary to remove

> a disincentive for the unemployed to become quickly reemployed in those States with low unemployment when the national trigger is on.[8]

Another Administration proposal (enacted) was for amending the unemployment compensation program for ex-service persons (UCX) by requiring states to disqualify from benefits any individual who voluntarily leaves the armed forces after serving an enlistment period. In effect, the amendment provides that if the individual could have reenlisted, but chose instead to leave the service and reenter the civilian work force, he will be considered a voluntary quit and denied benefits if he is unemployed and files for UI.[9]

These and other Reagan Administration proposals were recommended as a means of responding to what the DOL spokesman saw as a growing public image of beneficiaries,

> . . . who are prepared to ride the system until all benefits are exhausted, and who only then look for work.[10]

Implicit in the DOL testimony on behalf of reducing disincentives so as to encourage claimants to seek work was agreement with the image of claimants as preferring to draw benefits than accept jobs; a conviction that tests applied by state agencies of claimants' availability for work are inadequate; and a commitment to stricter eligibility and work search requirements rather than to making administration of existing requirements more effective and positive.

A change in attitudes toward claimants from sympathy to impatience was also demonstrated abundantly by Congress in the 1980 debates on new extended benefit standards, particularly on the requirement that a state have a waiting week for regular claimants as a condition for payment of the federal share of the cost for the first week of extended benefits. It was asserted that the waiting week would somehow encourage workers to seek jobs instead of filing for benefits immediately.[11] A skeptical view of claimants' job search determination was evident also in the debate concerning the deduction of retirement income from benefits. Such deduction, it was argued, was necessary to prevent retirees from draining the system.[12]

Allegations of excessive benefit costs and the prevailing suspicion of claimant motivations also seem to draw support from new revelations by behaviorists and economists showing that the average period of unemployment lengthens as benefit amounts or duration increase.[13] The implication is that as benefits become more "attractive" they lure more and more workers away from jobs. Many of these studies are solely statistical, without serious analysis of the implications of the figures or the validity of the samples used. If benefits are adequate, most unemployed workers are likely to spend a longer time trying to find the best job possible. Also, if benefits are adequate, more unemployed workers will file who ordinarily would delay because of embarrassment or unwillingness to become involved in the filing, registering, and reporting procedures. It is questionable, however, whether many individuals would deliberately forfeit a steady or even an uncertain job for benefits, amounting generally to half or less their regular weekly pay, for a period usually of half a year or less. The fact that most claimants do not exhaust their benefit entitlement even in hard times suggests the validity of the program's premise—that most people would rather work than draw benefits.

Finally, cost considerations and a predisposition to distrust benefit recipients seem also to encourage a certain inventiveness in developing justifications for proposed changes. The entire package of restrictive, cost-cutting 1981 Administration UI proposals, for example, was justified by Secretary of Labor Donovan in part on the grounds that their enactment "will strengthen this multi-billion dollar safety net for unemployed workers. . . ."[14]

Conclusions

This paper has been supportive of the balanced federal-state system and negative about the drift toward greater federal control over the program in recent years. Reasons for this view are explained later, but in the interest of balance, some mention should be made of the advantages and disadvantages of a single nationwide program of increased federal dominance.

Arguments for Federal Control

Perhaps the greatest advantage of a single national program is the opportunity it affords for equal treatment of claimants and employers throughout the country. In contrast, while state autonomy over program matters has permitted experimentation and innovation, it has also produced some serious inequalities. Some states provide the same treatment for all claimants except for those categories singled out by federal law for special treatment. Other states discriminate against interstate claimants, women, students, seasonal workers and part-time workers. In some states, disqualification provisions are so severe as to remove the offender completely from any protection under the program for the foreseeable future. Some states have enacted benefit formulas that fall far short of meeting any reasonable test of adequacy, and taxing provisions that are wholly unrealistic as means of ensuring solvency. State law differences, in many instances, result in claimants qualifying for wholly different UI benefits with identical base-period experience simply because they are in different states. Conversely, claimants with quite different work histories may qualify for identical benefit amounts and duration in different states. Divergent eligibility provisions produce situations in which a claimant in one state may be denied benefits for a certain act for six months or more, while in another state the same act may not be disqualifying at all. Employers with similar experience and payroll are regularly assigned wholly different tax rates in different states, depending on a great number of variables, and which may apply to different taxable wage bases as well.

Another advantage of a national system is financial. Nationwide pooling of all unemployment insurance taxes would require the maintenance of smaller reserves than the aggregate of 53 separate reserve funds. Such a system also has the potential to be a much more effective tool in controlling the economy. Federal domination should also lead to greater efficiency: The more uniformity throughout the country, the easier is the administrative burden. A national system also has the potential of unambiguous, united and effective leadership and direction, instead of 54 separate jurisdictions (53 "states" and one federal entity), each with authority over its own domain.

Nor is there any lack of support for a national or more federally dominated system. Both labor and, recently, business groups have supported greater federal control of the program. Organized labor has consistently favored benefit amount standards, as well as outright total federalization. It has also regularly looked to federal amendments to correct inadequacies and inequities of many states' programs. Labor representatives on the National Commission on Unemployment Compensation, for example, recommended that Con-

gress consider adding federal benefit standards in the following areas: the level of wage replacement represented by the
weekly benefit amount, qualifying requirements, waiting
periods, disqualifications, eligibility conditions for UI, appeals requirements, benefits for partial unemployment,
dependents' allowances, job search requirements and
assistance, rules for availability for work and active search
for work.[15]

Business groups have only recently acquired a fondness
for some federal standards. These former advocates of state
autonomy supported the Reagan Administration's 1981 proposals for several new federal standards in the extended
benefit area, and for a standard on a new suitable work
definition for regular benefit claimants. The Chamber of
Commerce, for example, recommended "swift enactment of
the President's Program for Economic Recovery, in its en-
tirety."

> As federal budget restrictions, the proposed
> changes in the UC program (see Appendix A) will
> contribute to national economic recovery. Most im-
> portantly, however, they are good for the UC pro-
> gram and constitute a modest step toward long
> overdue reform of the federal unemployment com-
> pensation laws.[16]

Similarly, the National Association of Manufacturers,
although it:

> . . . philosophically opposes any imposition of
> federal standards on individual State UC pro-
> grams, . . . urges you, the Congress, to respond to
> the Administration's proposed unemployment
> compensation savings in a courageous manner by
> expeditiously enacting the legislative proposals be-
> ing debated today.[17]

Both of these statements of support were for Administration proposals that included the "imposition . . . on individual State UC programs" of several new and sweeping federal standards. Traditional opposition by these organizations to enlarged federal control over the program apparently gives way in the face of opportunity for cost reduction and for a narrower definition of worker behavior acceptable as "deserving" of benefit support.

Disadvantages of Federal Dominance

A single national system that successfully provided uniformly fair and adequate UI provisions would be superior to the present federal-state system in the author's opinion. Unfortunately, a national system with the potential for eliminating inequalities and inequities also has the capability of doing the opposite. The capability for producing inequalities has been amply demonstrated. For example, state discriminatory provisions aimed at retirees, school employees, athletes, aliens, are federally mandated. That the federal government is as capable of inequities as any state is illustrated by the DOL-sponsored 1981 amendment and 1982 amendments to the federal program of unemployment compensation of ex-service persons (UCX) which required disqualification, as a voluntary quit without good cause, of anyone who left the service when he could have reenlisted. This questionable provision was dropped in 1982, but instead of reinstating the practice of treating veterans on an equal basis as other claimants, as was the case for over 20 years, Congress imposed a four week waiting period as a condition for benefits (not required of other claimants by any state) and established a ceiling of 13 weeks of benefits, half the usual 26 week maximums for regular benefits available in all but one state and one-third the usual maximum duration in states with extended benefits triggered on.[18]

The federal government is also no less capable than any state of absurdities, as illustrated by the 1982 requirement denying payment to any state of the federal share of the cost of extended benefits to the extent of "extra" benefit cost resulting from the state not rounding all the regular benefit amounts ending in other than full dollars, down to the next lower full dollar amount. There exists no viable means of effectively enforcing the provision. Finally, it should be noted that the federal government is as fully capable as any state of questionable judgment of the type illustrated by the severe 1981 restrictions (elimination of the national trigger, increase of insured unemployment rate levels required to activate state triggers, elimination of EB claimants from the computation of the trigger rates) imposed on the availability of extended benefits, at a time when record numbers of workers were losing their jobs—only to turn around within months and enact a special emergency program to help the long term unemployed, including those dropped from unemployment insurance protection solely because of the earlier amendments.

A 1978 General Accounting Office report of the UI system illustrates the dilemma, posed on the one hand by a hybrid federal-state system that produces inequalities but usually no nationwide blunders, and on the other hand by a national system (or a federally dominated partnership) that has the promise of equal treatment nationwide but also the potential for imposing provisions that are universally unfair or inadequate. In its report, the GAO recommended abolition of the extreme diversity of provisions it had discovered among the states:

> We recommend that the Congress establish uniform eligibility standards and methods for determining benefit amounts so that all UI claimants are treated equally.[19]

We believe that the benefit to be derived from our recommendation would outweigh what might be perceived by some as an intrusion on the partnership.[20]

Differences in eligibility and benefit provisions among the jurisdictions have a significant impact on program costs.[21]

The recommendation for greater uniformity "so that all UI claimants are treated equally" was not, however, accompanied by recommendations that would assure both uniformity and equity. Instead, GAO was disturbed that some states had no waiting week requirement, some did not deduct retirement income from benefits, some paid dependents' allowances, some permitted disqualified claimants to become eligible after a specified number of weeks rather than requiring them to requalify by getting another job. According to GAO estimates, these provisions increase UI costs over $1.0 billion.[22]

There was no discussion in the report of the merits of the provisions from the standpoint of program objectives or from any other standpoint than cost. The GAO completely ignored DOL's rebuttal that the very provisions the report singled out and implied were too expensive were provisions (except for dependents' allowances) the Department had urged the states to adopt for over 40 years, on the grounds that they provided fair treatment of claimants and made UI a more effective buffer against the hardships of unemployment. The GAO recommendations would thus have accomplished greater uniformity and saved money, but the cost of such "reforms" would be borne entirely by claimants and would be substantial.

Perhaps more important than other disadvantages of a national system is its potential for manipulating people. The recent amendments to the EB program, for example, seemed more aimed at forcing unemployed workers to seek any available job regardless of their skills, experience, former wage level or standard of living, than at providing meaningful help to people suffering from loss of jobs, income, and self-confidence. The concerted attacks in recent years by Administration spokesmen and Congressmen on the motivations and character of those receiving UI and other public entitlement program benefits seem deliberately intended to instill a sense of shame, or at least embarrassment, in recipients, and thereby to manipulate unemployed workers to forego or delay filing claims for benefits. Given the increasingly common attitude toward claimants as parasites rather than involuntarily unemployed workers, a wholly centralized, national program could become even more manipulative and oppressive.

Restoring a More Even Balance

The federal-state system has the disadvantages described earlier. But it does not have the same potential as a national system (or a federally dominated partnership) for manipulation. It still permits experimentation on an individual state basis; and with a constantly changing economy, the chance to test new ideas in individual state laboratories is needed as much now as 50 years ago. Unlike the mistakes of a national administration and Congress, which have nationwide implications and can be repealed only by another act of Congress, state disasters are usually confined to individual state borders, while successes can be quickly picked up by other states.

The current federal-state division of responsibilities is a source of the debate, discussion, conflict and confrontations discussed throughout this paper. These are the factors that have produced a unique vitality in a 45-year old program and that provide the key to its flexibility and responsiveness to new problems.

The means of retaining the advantages and preserving what is left of the federal-state balance lie in buttressing deterrents to federal takeover. The main reason for federal restraint in the past was widespread public acceptance and support of a system that seemed to work well and provided meaningful help to involuntarily unemployed workers. The general assumption was that the states maintained reasonably efficient, adequate programs at relatively low cost, and that benefits generally were paid only to workers unemployed through no fault of their own, most of whom were ready, willing and able to work. Given these assumptions (disturbed occasionally by a newspaper article or television program focusing on UI fraud or implying fraud), there was a natural reluctance to change a successful organizational structure.

The heavy unemployment of the mid-1970s, enactments during that period extending benefit duration to as much as 65 weeks, and the sudden and complete depletion of many states' reserves caused public reassessment not only of the capabilities of the states but also of the character of the UI claimant. The 1980 and 1981 federal invasions of state authority through a succession of program standards, motivated mostly by budget considerations, were made possible because of the erosion of public confidence in the system—encouraged and articulated by congressional and administration advocates of restrictive federal standards.

Restoration of past positive attitudes requires shoring up the current system's abilities to meet its basic responsibilities. First is the federal-state responsibility to ensure adequate financing of benefits.

The states must work their way back to solvency if public skepticism of their ability to manage their own UI programs is to be replaced by public confidence. States' heavy borrowing in recent years from a federal loan fund that itself has had to borrow from general revenues, has been interpreted as a sign of irresponsibility and a signal for federal takeover of state responsibilities. Federally imposed cost-saving measures have been substituted for state decisionmaking. The trend toward increased federal influence will certainly continue as long as substantial numbers of states must borrow "federal" money. The paths individual states must take to regain solvency and independence are many and varied and not the appropriate subject for this paper.

Clearly, states must take appropriate steps, but given the uneven impact among the states of recent recessions and the severe economic shocks suffered by some, it is no longer reasonable to expect individual states to carry the entire burden of extraordinary benefit costs. In some states, the most prudent financing measures conceivable would not have prevented complete depletion of state reserves. Some form of catastrophic reinsurance is clearly needed so that no state's reserves are so exhausted by a recession as to prevent it from recovering, through reasonable tax increases, within a relatively short period.

A second basic responsibility of the system is to ensure that benefits are paid only to those for whom the program is intended to help. If the public continues to believe that too many claimants would rather draw benefits than work, and that most states are either unable or unwilling to take necessary steps to limit benefits only to those genuinely eligible, more federal eligibility standards are likely to be forthcoming. The emphasis will continue to be on "stimulating work incentives" by tightening eligibility requirements, lowering benefits, and making disqualifications more severe, and it is possible that efforts will also be made to amend the law so as to permit (or require) states to limit benefits only to those who meet needs or income tests.

The UI program has always been vulnerable to charges that it is easy for claimants to cheat by not reporting all earnings for a week, by false statements about their availability for work, by insincere and half-hearted searches for a job. Everyone seems to know someone who has collected benefits apparently without being ready, willing and able to work. There is no question that some of the alleged abuse is real. Application of the availability and work search tests is the weakest aspect of UI administration.

Recent national administrations have tended to view abuse and fraud as common if not prevailing practices rather than aberrations. Instead of concentrating on making UI a more effective protection for individuals and their families, and a more effective counter-recessionary tool, they have focused on reducing abuse and providing new incentives to return to work, such as increasing the penalties for turning down a suitable job; considering as suitable any job the claimant is physically able to perform if it pays more than either the minimum wage or the claimant's weekly benefit amount; requiring that claimants produce tangible evidence of their work search efforts.

The disregard of such factors as the claimant's prior work experience, his skills and training and his past earnings levels only adds to employers' problems, since few individuals are likely to remain long in a job that is not compatible with their training and experience and out of line with their prior wage levels. It adds also to the problems of other unemployed individuals for whom the job, taken temporarily by the "over qualified" claimant, is suitable. The tangible evidence of work search requirement results in the claimant making employer contacts solely for the purpose of meeting the requirement—a futile effort by the claimant and a nuisance to employers.

A better approach, tried on an experimental basis from time to time, is a positive, thorough application of each state's existing availability for work and work search requirements. Such an approach requires individualized treatment of each claimant to the greatest feasible extent. It involves joint employment service and UI evaluation of the claimant's prospects for local reemployment in his usual occupation and his need and aptitude for acquiring new skills that are in demand. Most important, for claimants not expecting recall to their jobs, it requires the early cooperative development by the employment service and UI staff with the claimant of a plan representing the most realistic path to the claimant's reemployment in suitable work; actual implementation of the plan and adjustment of the plan when necessary; and a periodic evaluation of the claimant's own pursuit of the plan and of his availability for work.[23] This approach is expensive, but it may be cost effective if all social as well as program costs are taken into account. It represents the most productive and realistic approach possible, from the standpoint of the claimant, the state agency, and employers.

The effective application of a thorough reemployment service would also permit the early indentification of those individuals not really committed to working. Accordingly, this approach would seem to be the most effective means of reducing abuse of the program by claimants. It should also help in restoring public confidence in state ability to limit benefit payments only to those who genuinely meet the state eligibility conditions.

A third basic responsibility of the system is to provide adequate benefits. A sure invitation to increased federal control of the program is for the states to continue to fall short of this goal. Federal benefit standards have received considerable support in the past primarily because states neglected to prescribe reasonable benefit levels. Clearly such standards are not likely in the immediate future. However, the current federal emphasis on cutting costs will in time be replaced by a genuine concern for the plight of unemployed workers. It will be accompanied by a growing conviction that a state UI program should be expected to meet some reasonable benchmark of minimum benefit adequacy to qualify the state's employers for credit against the federal tax. Unless the states do this voluntarily, it will be done for them.

A fourth basic responsibility is for the system to reestablish reasonable program objectives and goals. This means resumption by the federal partner of its responsibility for developing and recommending provisions for state consideration based on criteria of fairness and adequacy, as well as cost. Resumption of its traditional advocacy role (by a DOL genuinely committed to strengthening UI) would provide a needed focus on program improvement, abandoned to cost considerations in recent years. It would represent a return by the federal partner to a role of leadership in establishing broad as well as specific program goals and in persuading states of the merits of its recommendations on the basis of reason, research and experience, rather than coercion.

If adopted, these four general recommendations should help renew public confidence in unemployment insurance. Their adoption should lead to greater support for the program's original objectives and a change in the current public image of the claimant as lazy, devious and undeserving. These changes in the public perceptions would seem to be prerequisite to restoring the traditional federal-state balance of power. In addition, if the old partnership is to be revived, it seems necessary that there also be greater public awareness of the hazards of centralized control and the values of a pluralistic system. Perhaps this monograph will contribute to that end.

NOTES

1. Testimony by representatives of the Interstate Conference of Employment Security Agencies on recent amendments has been a mixture of support for restrictive EB standards (e.g., changes in EB triggers) and opposition to proposals for restrictive regular program standards (e.g., new suitable work criteria after 13 weeks).

2. Peter Henle, "The Federal Budget: Removal of State Unemployment Trust Funds," *Unemployment Compensation: Studies and Research,* Vol. 2 (Washington: National Commission on Unemployment Compensation, 1980), pp. 373-387.

3. *Unemployment Compensation: Final Report* (National Commission on Unemployment Compensation, July 1980), p. 104.

4. Information about state UI loans and general U.S. Treasury advances based on data supplied by the UIS.

5. For discussion of Michigan's UI fund crisis and options for meeting the problem, see Saul J. Blaustein, *Unemployment Insurance Fund Insolvency and Debt in Michigan* (Kalamazoo, MI: W. E. Upjohn Institute for Employment Research, September 1982).

6. P.L. 96-499, approved December 5, 1980, amended the Federal-State Extended Unemployment Compensation Act of 1970. See chapter 3 for discussion of extended benefit standard on suitable work and work search.

7. Statement of Raymond J. Donovan, Secretary of Labor, before the Subcommittee on Public Assistance and Unemployment Compensation, Committee on Ways and Means, U.S. House of Representatives, March 12, 1981. DOL's proposals incorporated in S. 983, introduced by Senator Dole, and H.R. 2880, introduced by Congressman Conable. Proposal not enacted.

8. Statement of Lawrence E. Weatherford, Acting Deputy Assistant Secretary for Employment and Training, U.S. Department of Labor, before the Subcommittee on Public Assistance and Unemployment Compensation, Committee on Ways and Means, U.S. House of Representatives, March 12, 1981. Proposal enacted as part of P.L. 97-35, approved August 13, 1981.

9. P.L. 97-35, approved August 13, 1981.

10. Weatherford, *op. cit.*

11. *Congressional Record* (March 4, 1980), Senator Boren, pp. S 2104-2105.

12. *Ibid.*

13. See, for example, Daniel Hamermesh, *Jobless Pay and the Economy* (The Johns Hopkins University Press, 1977), pp. 32ff; and Stephen T. Marston, "Voluntary Unemployment," in *Unemployment Compensation: Studies and Research,* Vol. 2 (Washington: National Commission on Unemployment Compensation, 1980), pp. 431-438.

14. Donovan, *op. cit.*

15. *Unemployment Compensation: Final Report, op. cit.,* p. 190.

16. Statement on Proposed Budget Reductions in the Unemployment Compensation Program before the Subcommittee on Public Assistance and Unemployment Compensation of the House Committee on Ways and Means, for the Chamber of Commerce of the United States, by Samuel E. Dyer, March 11, 1981.

17. Testimony on behalf of the National Association of Manufacturers on the Administration's Proposed Savings on Unemployment Compensation before the Subcommittee on Public Assistance and Unemployment Compensation of the Ways and Means Committee, U.S. House of Representatives, March 11, 1981.

18. P.L. 97-362.

19. United States General Accounting Office, Report to the Congress by the Comptroller General, *Unemployment Insurance—Need to Reduce Unequal Treatment of Claimants and Improve Benefit Payment Controls and Tax Collections,* April 5, 1978, p. 21.

20. *Ibid.,* p. 23.

21. *Ibid.,* p. 7.

22. *Ibid.,* p. 8.

23. The same intensive, periodic, individualized application of the availability and work search requirements is advocated by Saul J. Blaustein in *Job and Income Security for Unemployed Workers* (Kalamazoo, MI: W. E. Upjohn Institute for Employment Research, 1981): "Emphasis is always on encouragement and assistance to the claimant in finding employment. The expectation underlying this emphasis is that the true attitudes of the claimant with regard to desire and availability for work are more readily revealed in the context of a positive approach than in a direct attempt at the outset to question the claimant's labor force attachment and behavior." Pp. 27, 28.